CAMBRIDGE
UNIVERSITY PRESS

ICT Starters

Next Steps Stage 2

Victoria Ellis, Sarah Lawrey and Doug Dickinson

CAMBRIDGE
UNIVERSITY PRESS

University Printing House, Cambridge CB2 8BS, United Kingdom

One Liberty Plaza, 20th Floor, New York, NY 10006, USA

477 Williamstown Road, Port Melbourne, VIC 3207, Australia

314–321, 3rd Floor, Plot 3, Splendor Forum, Jasola District Centre, New Delhi – 110025, India

103 Penang Road, #05-06/07, Visioncrest Commercial, Singapore 238467

Cambridge University Press is part of the University of Cambridge.

It furthers the University's mission by disseminating knowledge in the pursuit of education, learning and research at the highest international levels of excellence.

www.cambridge.org
Information on this title: www.cambridge.org/9781108463539

© Cambridge University Press 2019

This publication is in copyright. Subject to statutory exception and to the provisions of relevant collective licensing agreements, no reproduction of any part may take place without the written permission of Cambridge University Press.

First published 2003
Second edition 2005
Third edition 2013
Fourth edition 2019

20 19 18 17 16 15 14 13

Printed in Poland by Opolgraf

A catalogue record for this publication is available from the British Library

ISBN 978-1-108-46353-9 Paperback

Additional resources for this publication are available through Cambridge GO. Visit cambridge.org/go

Cambridge University Press has no responsibility for the persistence or accuracy of URLs for external or third-party internet websites referred to in this publication, and does not guarantee that any content on such websites is, or will remain, accurate or appropriate. Information regarding prices, travel timetables, and other factual information given in this work is correct at the time of first printing but Cambridge University Press does not guarantee the accuracy of such information thereafter.

All exam-style questions and sample answers in this title were written by the authors. In examinations, the way marks are awarded may be different.

....

NOTICE TO TEACHERS IN THE UK
It is illegal to reproduce any part of this work in material form (including photocopying and electronic storage) except under the following circumstances:
(i)   where you are abiding by a licence granted to your school or institution by the Copyright Licensing Agency;
(ii) where no such licence exists, or where you wish to exceed the terms of a licence, and you have gained the written permission of Cambridge University Press;
(iii) where you are allowed to reproduce without permission under the provisions of Chapter 3 of the Copyright, Designs and Patents Act 1988, which covers, for example, the reproduction of short passages within certain types of educational anthology and reproduction for the purposes of setting examination questions.

Introduction

Cambridge ICT Starters: Next Steps Stage 2 has been written to support you in your work for the Cambridge International Diploma ICT Starters syllabus (Next Steps) from 2019. This book provides full coverage of all of the modules so that you will have a good platform of skills and information to support you in the next stages of your development of ICT capability. The modules can be studied in any order. The book supports your work on the key skills and basic routines needed at this level to become competent in emailing, handling data, basic spreadsheet management, creating and editing written work and handling images.

The book provides you and your helpers with:

- examples of activities to do
- exercises to practise the skills before you put them into practice
- final projects to show just how much you have learnt
- optional scenario and challenge activities for those who want to challenge themselves further.

It is designed for use in the classroom with help and support from trained teachers. The tasks, skills and activities have been set in real situations where computer access will be essential. At the start of each module there is a section called 'Before you start …' that explains what you need to know before you begin. The activities are designed to lead you towards a final project where you will have the opportunity to display your knowledge and understanding of each of the skills.

Some exercises require you to open prepared files for editing. These files are available to be downloaded by your teachers from cambridge.org/go. You will find that the website provides the files to get you started. These files are included to help you start the activities in this book.

The modules in this book use Microsoft Office 2016, Scratch, Gmail and a variety of web browsers and search engines. Using these will develop your digital skills and will mean that the notes and activities in the book will be easy for you to follow. However, your teacher may decide to use different applications to help you to meet the module objectives.

We hope you enjoy working on this stage and will take pleasure in your learning.

Good luck!

Contents

Next Steps 2
Introduction

1. Exploring programming 6
2. Exploring the internet 43
3. Exploring email 62
4. Exploring multimedia 90

How to use this book

How to use this book

In every module, look out for these features:

Module objectives: This table shows you the key things that you will learn in this module.

	In this module, you will learn how to:	Pass/Merit	Done?
1	Plan an algorithm to draw a simple repeating shape or pattern	P	
2	Create a program to produce a simple repeating shape or pattern	P	
3	Predict the output of a program that includes repetition.	P	

Key words: These boxes provide you with definitions of words that may be important or useful.

> **Key word**
>
> **Algorithm:**
> a series of steps that are followed.

Did you know?: These boxes provide interesting information and opportunities for further research.

> **Did you know?**
>
> The World Wide Web was invented in 1989 by Tim Berners-Lee. The first website was created in 1990.

Tip: These boxes give you handy hints as you work.

> **Tip**
>
> You can change the size of your Sprite.

Watch out!: These boxes help you to avoid making mistakes in your work.

> **WATCH OUT!**
>
> Only use 'Reply all' if you want to send your message to everyone.

Challenge: These activities are more difficult and extend beyond the syllabus.

> **Challenge**

Scenario: These are tasks that help you practise everything you have learnt in the module in a "real-life" situation.

> **Scenario**
>
> **Out of this world!**

Pass/Merit: This shows you the level of all of the activities in the book.

> **Skill 6**

Skill box: These boxes contain activities for you to test what you have learnt.

> **Skill 1**

Stay safe!: These boxes contain e-safety advice.

> **Stay safe!**
>
> Only search for appropriate topics on the internet, and if you see anything you are unsure of tell your teacher.

Exploring programming 1

	In this module, you will learn how to:	Pass/Merit	Done?
1	Plan an algorithm to draw a simple repeating shape or pattern	P	
2	Create a program to produce a simple repeating shape or pattern	P	
3	Predict the output of a program that includes repetition	P	
4	Plan an algorithm to draw a complex shape or pattern, using decomposition	M	
5	Create a procedure and use it in a program to draw a complex shape or pattern.	M	

In this module you are going to develop skills to help you create a sign for Shamim's sweet shop using Scratch. Shamim wants you to create her lollipop sign in Scratch. You will learn how to split the sign down into smaller parts and draw shapes in Scratch with the pen tool. At the end you will combine all your new skills to create her lollipop sign.

You will learn how to use **repetition** and **procedures** to produce an efficient program by combining shapes to produce a lollipop image. You will do this by **decomposing** the task into smaller parts: the smaller the tasks, the easier they are to solve.

You will also learn how to:

- use the pen to draw lines and shapes
- change the colour and pen size of the pen.

Did you know?

Repetition is one of the three core programming building blocks. The other two are: sequence and selection.

Key words

Repetition: doing the same thing more than once.

Procedure: a set of instructions that is separate from the main program: these instructions can be used repeatedly.

Decomposition: splitting a problem down into a set of smaller problems.

1 Exploring programming

Before you start

You should:

- have had some experience of using Scratch to control a Sprite, for example, to make it move and turn at specific angles
- be able to save and open programs produced in Scratch
- know what a flowchart is and how it is used to plan a program
- have created and followed flowcharts
- be familiar with angles, and calculating the angles of shapes.

Introduction

Scratch is a piece of software that allows you to write simple programs to control characters called Sprites. You write programs by inserting code blocks that let you edit pieces of data such as how far forward you want your character to move.

Skill 1

What is repetition?

Repetition is the repeating of an action. For example, when washing the dishes:

1. Pick up a dish.
2. Put the dish in the sink.
3. Wash the dish.
4. Put the dish to dry.
5. Repeat steps 1–4 until there are no dishes left.

This is called a **repeat loop**.

Repetition makes programs efficient. You could keep writing…

1. Pick up a dish.
2. Put the dish in the sink.
3. Wash the dish.
4. Put the dish to dry.

> **Key word**
>
> **Repeat loop:** a command that tells you to do something more than once.

5 Pick up a dish.

6 Put the dish in the sink.

7 Wash the dish.

8 Put dish to dry.

9 …and so on.

…but this wastes code, and how do you know how many dishes you have? Every time you need to wash the dishes, you will have to rewrite the program.

Activity 1.1

Repeat the following four times:

1 Stand up.

2 Turn around.

3 Sit down.

How many times did you stand up? This matches the number of times you repeated the task.

Rewrite the **algorithm** so it repeats six times.

Activity 1.2

1 Pick up a pen.

2 Put it back down.

3 Pick up a pen.

4 Put it back down.

5 Pick up a pen.

6 Put it back down.

How many times did you repeat this action?

Rewrite these instructions using 'Repeat'.

_____

_____

> **Key word**
>
> **Algorithm:** a series of steps that are followed.

1 Exploring programming

Activity 1.3

You need a pencil and a piece of graph paper. Follow the instructions below, starting in the bottom left-hand corner of the paper. The first two steps are shown in the image.

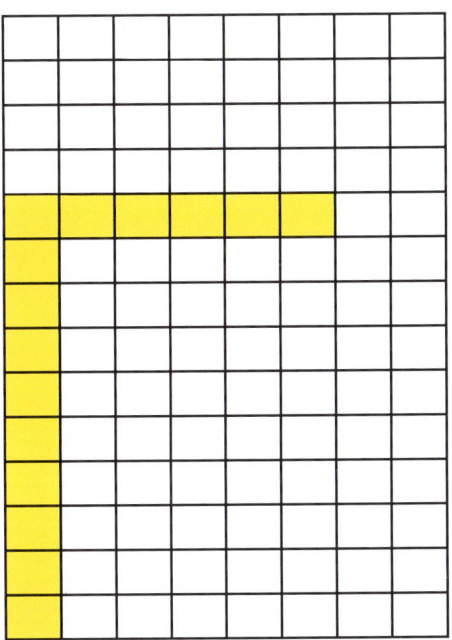

1. Colour in 10 squares up.
2. Colour in 5 squares to the right.
3. Colour in 10 squares up.
4. Colour in 5 squares to the right.
5. Colour in 10 squares up.
6. Colour in 5 squares to the right.
7. Colour in 10 squares up.
8. Colour in 5 squares to the right.

How many times did you repeat an action?

Rewrite these instructions using 'Repeat'.

> **Tip**
> You will need to start at the bottom left of your piece of graph paper.

Skill 2

Planning an algorithm using repetition

A flowchart is a diagram that helps you plan an algorithm. You will need to plan the lollipop sign before you create it.

A flowchart has set shapes that you combine with arrows to show the structure of the program.

Key word

Decision: a question where you have to make a choice, either 'Yes' or 'No'.

The image shows the four symbols used in a flowchart.

You should already be familiar with 'Start', 'Stop' and 'Process'.

Decision is a choice and it has two arrows coming from it, one for 'Yes' and one 'No'.

The Decision box has a question inside it. The question can only have 'Yes', or 'No' as an answer, for example:

- Has it repeated four times?
- Has the user clicked 'Stop'?

Here is an example:

Repeat four times:

1. Stand up.
2. Turn around.
3. Sit down.

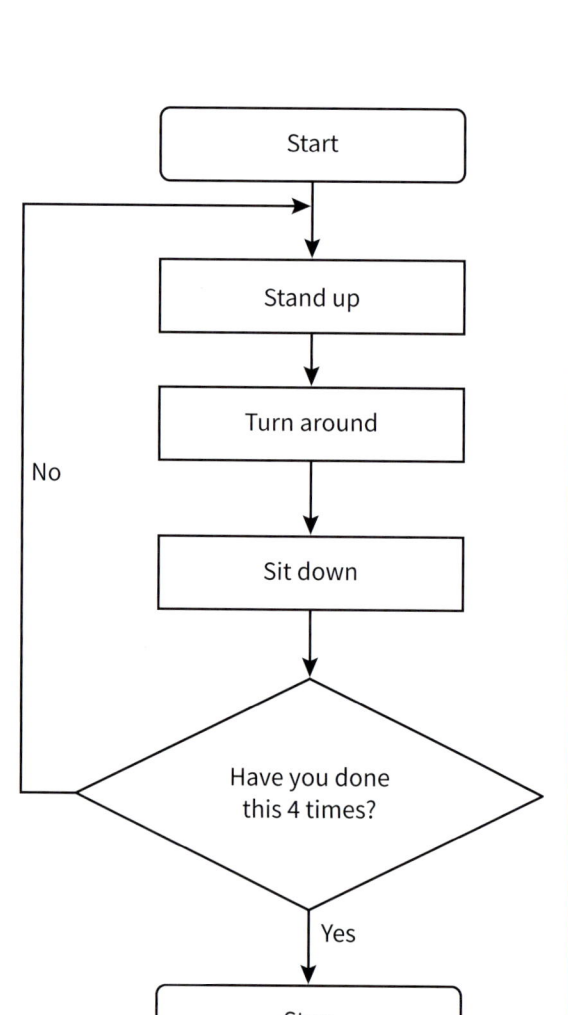

1 Exploring programming

Read the flowchart following the arrows.

When you get to the question, if you have completed the actions four times then follow the 'Yes' arrow.

If you haven't, follow the 'No' arrow.

You can also put the question at the start.

Here is a flowchart telling a Scratch Sprite to move forward, then turn left 90 degrees four times.

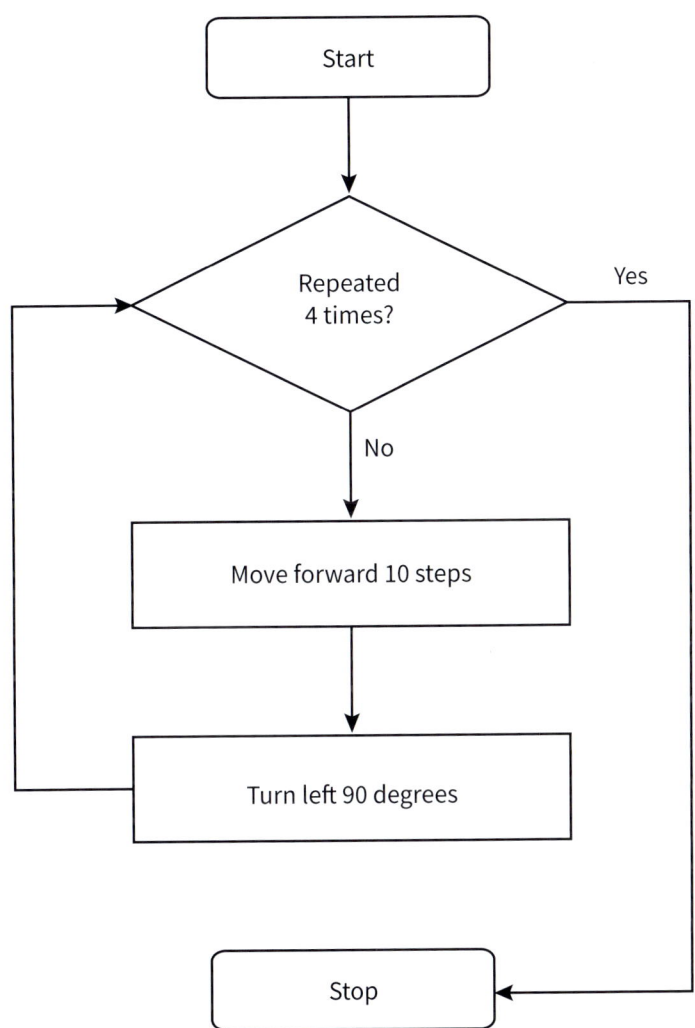

Activity 2.1
Follow the instructions on the flowchart:

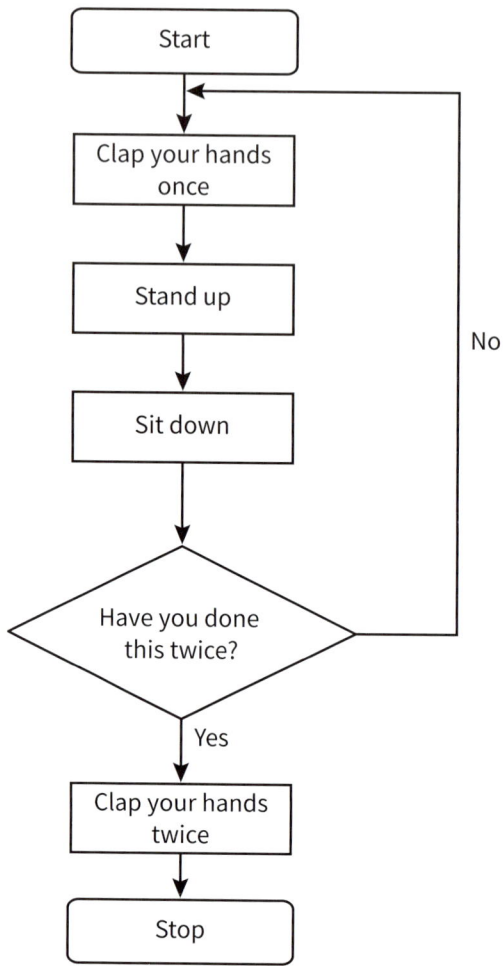

Activity 2.2
Follow this algorithm:

Repeat five times:

1 Put your right hand on your head.
2 Put your left hand on your head.
3 Put both hands on the table.

Draw a flowchart for this algorithm using repetition.

Activity 2.3
A character needs to move forward 20 steps, then turn right 45 degrees. It needs to do this ten times.

Draw a flowchart for this algorithm using repetition.

1 Exploring programming

Skill 3

Using repetition in Scratch

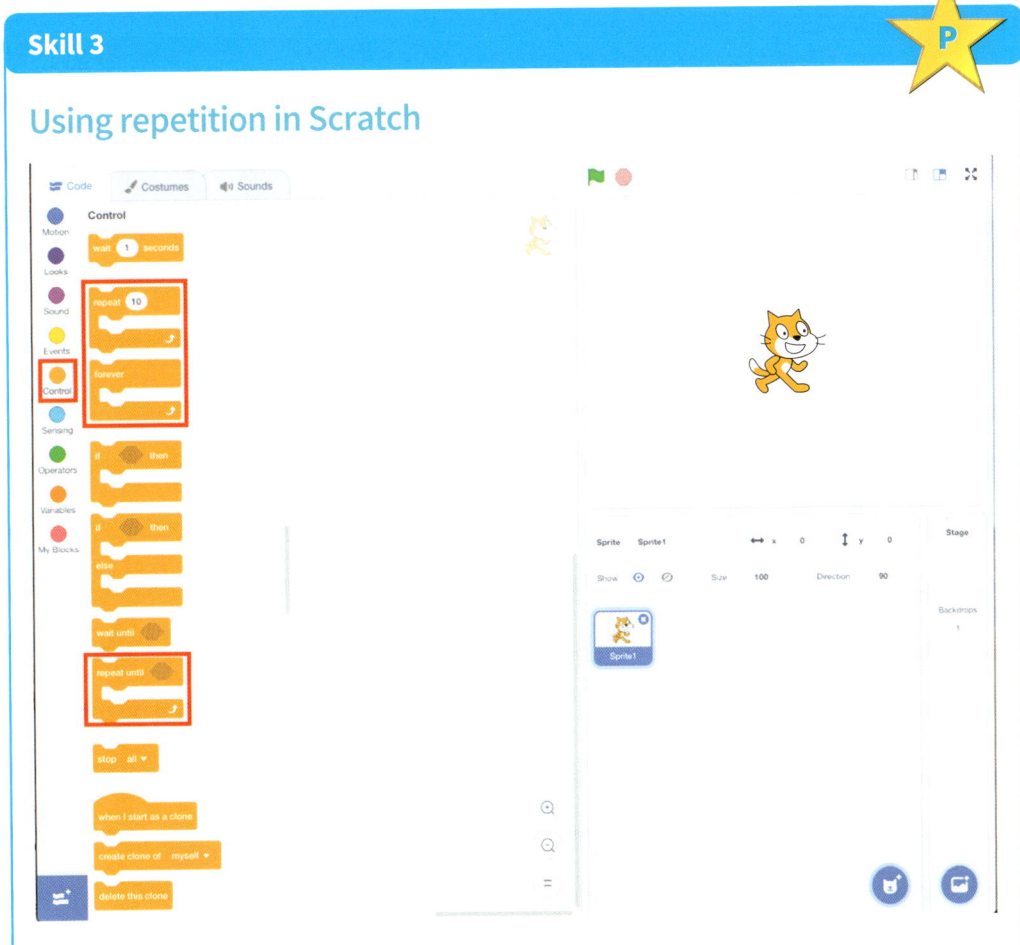

Click on the **Control** menu in Scratch. There are three different repetition statements in Scratch. You only need to use the first two.

The first repetition statement will run the code the number of times in the white box. This one will run ten times.

To change the number, simply click in it and enter the new number.

The second repetition statement will run the code inside it forever. It will not stop until the program is stopped.

13

> **Tip**
> You can change the size of your Sprite.

Click on the **Size** button and change the number to make your Sprite larger or smaller.

Size 100

Activity 3.1
Start an algorithm with the  block.

You will find this in **Events**.

Add a  from **Control**.

Change the 10 to a 5. This will make the code repeat five times.

Select  from the **Motion** menu inside the repetition statement.

The code should look like this:

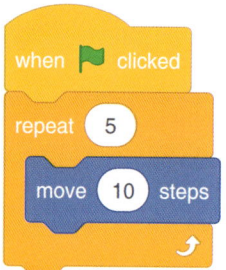

Run the program.

The Sprite should have moved forward 10 steps, five times (a total of 50 steps). It will look as if it has done this all at once as the Sprite performs very quickly.

Activity 3.2
Create a program that performs the following algorithm.

Repeat twice:

1 Move 100 steps.
2 Turn left 90 degrees.

1 Exploring programming

Activity 3.3

You can put blocks before a 'Repeat' statement.

Create a program that performs the following algorithm:

- Move 100 steps.
- Repeat four times:
  1 Turn left 90 degrees.
  2 Move 50 steps.

Run the program. If the program moves too fast, you can put 'Wait' commands between blocks, for example:

Activity 3.4

You can put blocks after a 'Repeat' statement.

Create a program that performs the following algorithm:

- Move 50 steps.
- Turn left 45 degrees.
- Repeat three times:
  1 Turn left 120 degrees.
  2 Move 100 steps.
- Turn left 45 degrees.
- Move 50 steps.

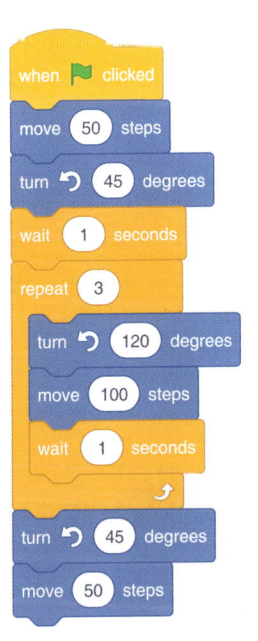

Tip

Don't forget to put the 'Wait' block in to slow down the program.

Skill 4

To draw a shape, you need to use the pen in Scratch. You will need to use the pen to draw the shapes in the lollipop sign for Shamim's sweet shop.

Using the pen

You can use your Sprite to draw an image on the screen.

The pen tool is found in the **Codes** list by clicking on the **Extensions** button.

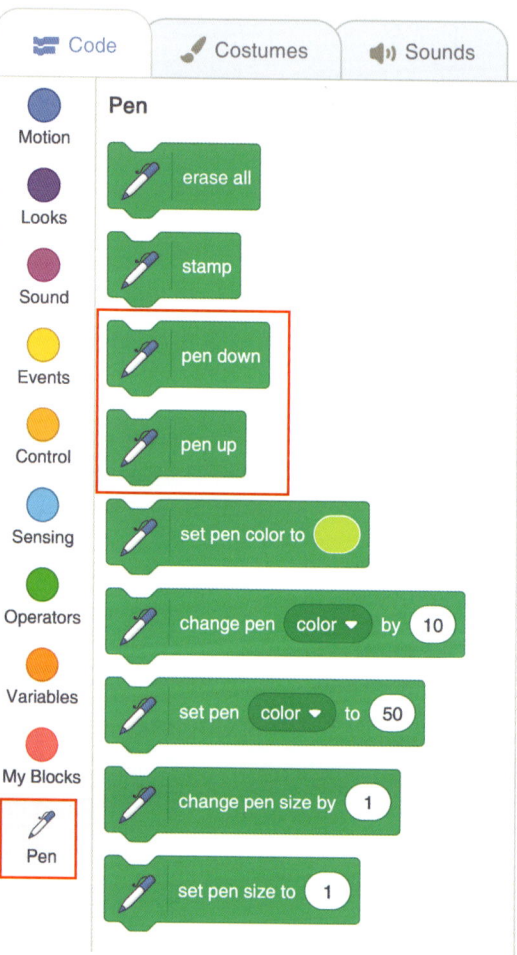

Choose the **Pen** category.

The pen down block tells the Sprite to start drawing.

1 Exploring programming

The [pen up] block tells the Sprite to stop drawing.

Use [erase all] at the start of each program if you want to remove any previous lines, for example:

> **Key word**
>
> **Erase all:** remove everything that was there before.

Activity 4.1

Make the Sprite draw a straight line 100 steps long.

Put in a 'pen down' block, and then move 100 steps.

Run the program; the Sprite should have left a line behind it.

Activity 4.2

Have a go at drawing a line.

Make the Sprite perform the following algorithm:

- Put the pen down.
- Move forward 100 steps.
- Turn left 90 degrees.
- Move forward 50 steps.
- Turn left 90 degrees.
- Move forward 50 steps.
- Turn right 90 degrees.
- Move forward 50 steps.
- Turn left 90 degrees.
- Move forward 50 steps.
- Put the pen up.

Activity 4.3

Make the Sprite perform the following algorithm:

- Put the pen down.
- Repeat 5 times:
    1. Turn left 90 degrees.
    2. Move forward 50 steps.
    3. Turn right 90 degrees.
    4. Move forward 50 steps.
- Put the pen up.

Tip

Put 'Wait' blocks in if you want to see each Sprite move.

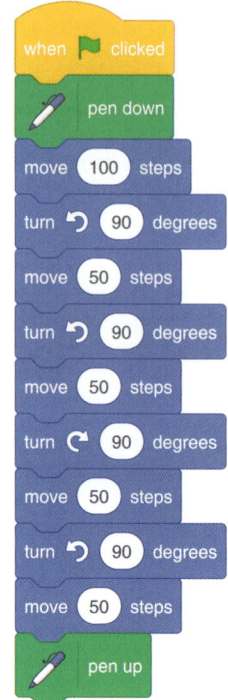

1 Exploring programming

Skill 5

Working with shapes

The lollipop sign is made up of smaller shapes.

Shapes can have different numbers of sides and different angles.

An angle is the degree that you have to turn.

This shows common angles if you are turning to the right.

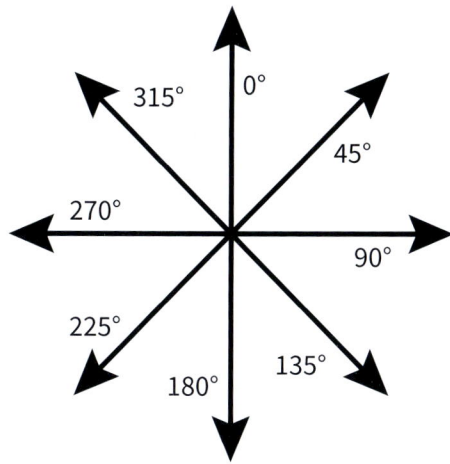

These are reversed if you are turning to the left.

If you make several turns, to end up facing the same direction that you started, all the turns must add up to 360 degrees.

To measure angles you need a protractor.

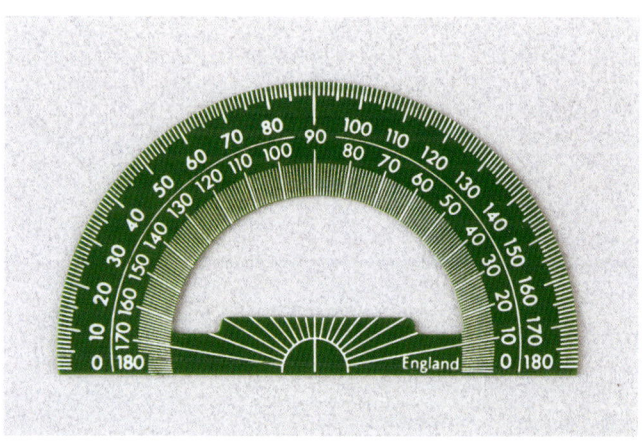

Now you can work out the size of the angle that the Sprite needs to turn in order to follow the line from beginning to end.

The Sprite moves forward 100. It then reaches a bend. It needs to turn to continue following the line.

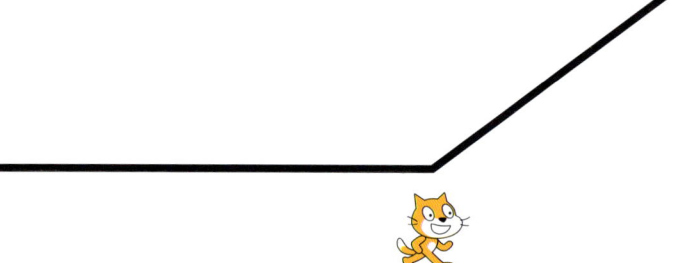

You can draw a line as though the Sprite was going to continue straight ahead. You can call this the 'projected line'.

Will the Sprite need to turn left or right?

You can measure the angle between the pretend line and where it needs to turn to.

This is the amount of turn (angle) that the Sprite would need to make.

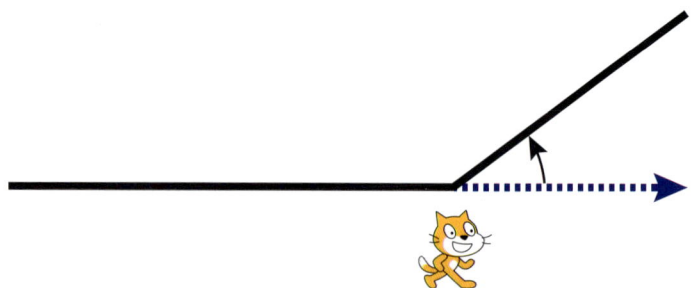

1 Exploring programming

Activity 5.1
Will the Sprite need to turn left or right?

Measure the angle you will need to turn to follow the line.

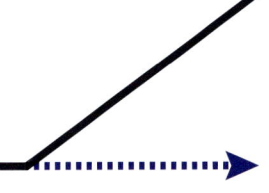

Tip

Draw the pretend line. Then measure the angle between the two lines.

Activity 5.2
Will the Sprite need to turn left or right?

Measure the angle you will need to turn to follow the line.

Activity 5.3

There are two bends in this line.

For each one, decide if the Sprite needs to turn left or right.

Measure each angle you will need to turn to follow the line to the end.

Activity 5.4

The Sprite is now going in the opposite direction.

For each angle, decide if the Sprite needs to turn left or right.

Measure each angle you will need to turn to follow the line to the end.

Skill 6

Drawing a regular shape using repetition

Repetition can be used to draw a shape, for example a square.

You need to know the angle in each corner of the shape, for example a square has 90 degree corners.

Calculating the angles

A complete circle is 360 degrees.

Divide 360 by the number of sides in a shape to get the external angle.

1 Exploring programming

For example:

A square has four sides: 360 / 4 = 90 degrees

An equilateral has three sides: 360 / 3 = 120 degrees

A square can be drawn using the commands:

- Forward 100.
- Turn left 90.
- Forward 100.
- Turn left 90.
- Forward 100.
- Turn left 90.
- Forward 100.
- Turn left 90.

The two commands 'Forward 100' and 'Turn left 90' are repeated four times (the number of sides). This can be simplified to:

Repeat four times:

1. Forward 100.
2. Turn left 90.

Activity 6.1

Look back at **Skill 2** to remind yourself about flowcharts.

Draw a flowchart to produce a square. Each side should be 100 steps long.

Activity 6.2

Use your flowchart from **Activity 6.1** to create a Scratch program to draw a square.

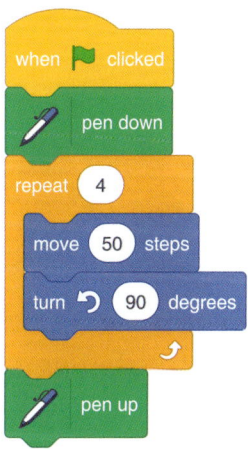

> **Tip**
> Remember that the / symbol means 'divide'.

> **Tip**
> Remember that in Scratch, Forward means Move.

> **Tip**
> Think about how many times it needs to repeat? What angle does it need to turn?

> **Tip**
> Use the 'pen down' block to draw the shape.

Tip

To work out the angle to turn, divide 360 by the number of sides in a shape.

Tip

A triangle has three sides, so it will need to repeat three times.

Tip

If you can't see your shape, you can use Scratch blocks to make your Sprite hide (so it is invisible) and show (to make it visible). 'show' and 'hide' are in the **Looks** menu;

put 'show' at the start of your program, then 'hide' at the end:

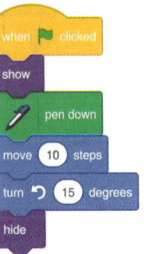

Activity 6.3

A triangle has three sides.

Work out the size of each angle in an equilateral triangle.

Draw a flowchart to produce a triangle with sides 100 steps long using repetition.

Activity 6.4

Use your flowchart from **Activity 6.3** to create a Scratch program to draw a triangle.

Activity 6.5

An octagon has eight sides.

Draw a flowchart to produce an octagon with sides 50 steps long.

Activity 6.6

Use your flowchart from **Activity 6.5** to create a Scratch program to draw an octagon.

Activity 6.7

You can draw a circle by turning 1 degree each time.

Work out the length of each step forward and how many times you need to turn 1 degree to complete a whole circle.

Draw a flowchart to draw a circle with 2 steps between each turn.

Create a Scratch program to draw the circle.

If you need to restart your program, add these blocks to your code.

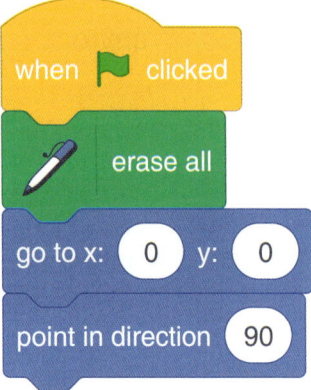

This means when you click on your Sprite in the program, it will remove all lines, turn to face the right of the screen and return to the starting position so it's ready to start again!

1 Exploring programming

Skill 7

Drawing a new shape, using repetition

Shapes are not always **regular**, for example, a rectangle.

The sides have different lengths but there is still repetition.

The algorithm to draw this rectangle without repetition is:

- Forward 200.
- Left 90.
- Forward 50.
- Left 90.
- Forward 200.
- Left 90.
- Forward 50.
- Left 90.

The first four commands are repeated twice. This can be written in Scratch as:

Repeat two times:

1. Forward 200.
2. Left 90.
3. Forward 50.
4. Left 90.

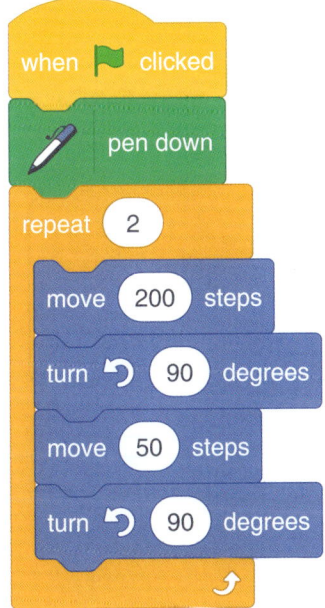

Key word

Regular: all the sides and angles are exactly the same.

Activity 7.1

This shape

can be drawn with the algorithm:

- Forward 200 steps.
- Turn left 45 degrees.
- Forward 50 steps.
- Turn left 90 degrees.
- Forward 50 steps.
- Turn left 45 degrees.
- Forward 200 steps.
- Turn left 45 degrees.
- Forward 50 steps.
- Turn left 90 degrees.
- Forward 50 steps.
- Turn left 45 degrees.

Create a Scratch program to produce the shape using repetition.

Activity 7.2

Create an algorithm in Scratch to draw this shape using repetition.

Tip

Revisit **Activity 6.7** to add blocks to restart your program.

Tip

There should be two repetitions. Find the code that repeats.

Tip

There are four repetitions. All the angles are the same.

1 Exploring programming

Skill 8

Predicting the outcome of a program that uses repetition

To predict what a program will do, you need to follow the algorithm or flowchart without running the program. Follow each step and either:

1. imagine what it will do, or
2. draw what it will do on a piece of paper.

Activity 8.1

Predict what shape the flowchart will produce.

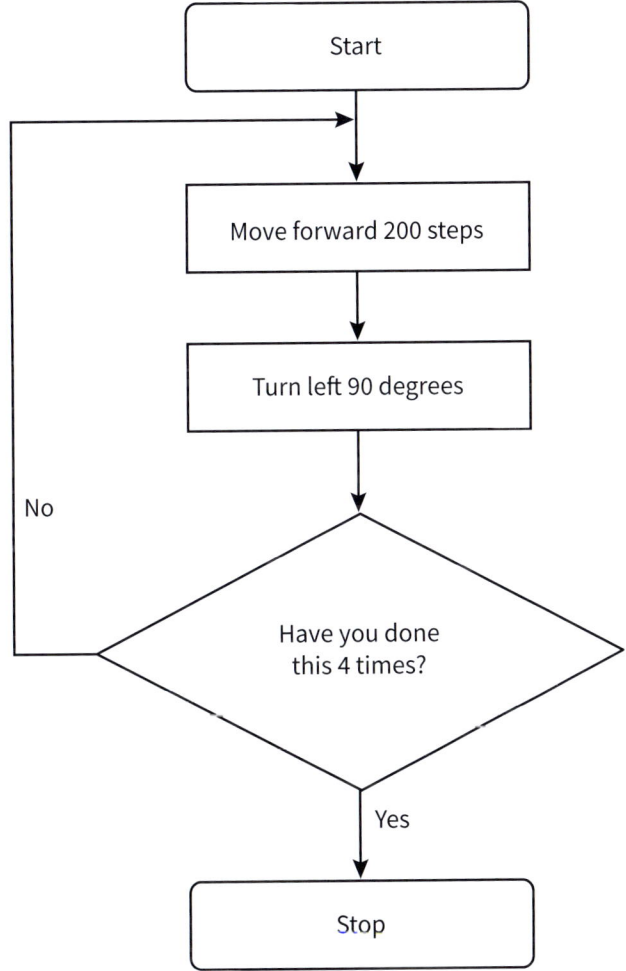

Create a Scratch program for the flowchart. Were you correct?

Activity 8.2
Predict what shape the flowchart will produce.

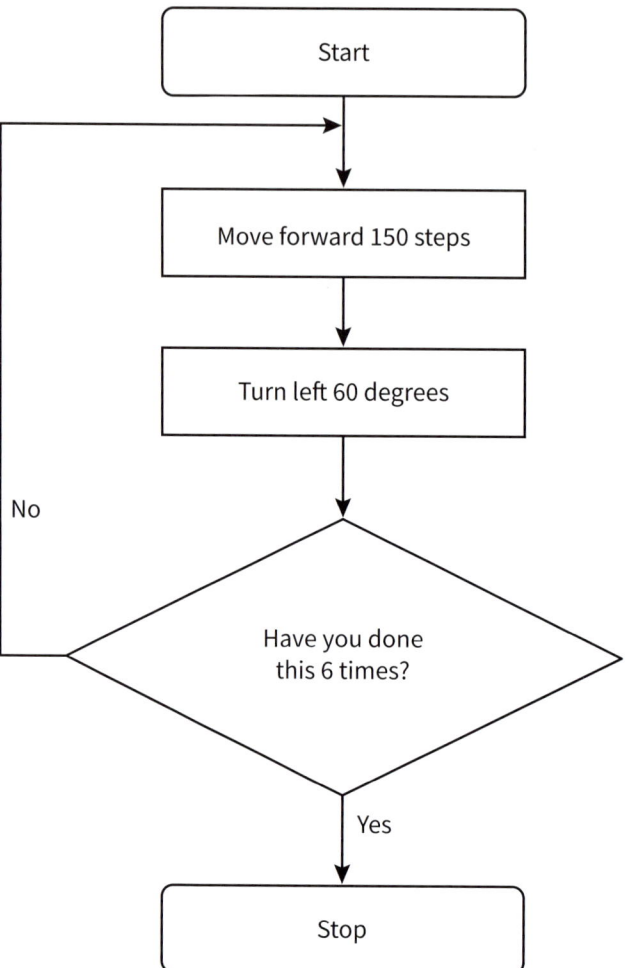

Create a Scratch program for the flowchart. Were you correct?

1 Exploring programming

Activity 8.3
Predict what shape the flowchart will produce.

```
          Start
            │
            ▼
    ┌───────────────┐
───▶│ Move forward  │
│   │   50 steps    │
│   └───────────────┘
│           │
│           ▼
│   ┌───────────────┐
│   │ Turn left 144 │
│   │   degrees     │
│No └───────────────┘
│           │
│           ▼
│   ┌───────────────┐
│   │ Move forward  │
│   │   50 steps    │
│   └───────────────┘
│           │
│           ▼
│   ┌───────────────┐
│   │ Turn right 72 │
│   │   degrees     │
│   └───────────────┘
│           │
│           ▼
│        ◇─────◇
│       ╱  Have  ╲
└──────╱ you done ╲
       ╲ this 5   ╱
        ╲ times? ╱
         ◇─────◇
            │ Yes
            ▼
          Stop
```

> **Tip**
>
> You might want to use the protractor shown in **Skill 5** to help work out the angles.

Create a Scratch program for the flowchart. Were you correct?

Skill 9

Procedures

A procedure is a set of instructions that are separate from the main program. In Scratch these are also known as custom blocks.

You can then call this procedure as many times as you like in the main program and the code in it will run each time.

This is part of the **abstraction** of a problem. Abstraction is an important part of programming. It is when you simplify a problem so it can be programmed for a computer.

To create a procedure you open Scratch and click on **My Blocks**, and then **Make a Block**.

This window will open.

> **Key word**
>
> **Abstraction:** simplify a problem by removing unnecessary parts.

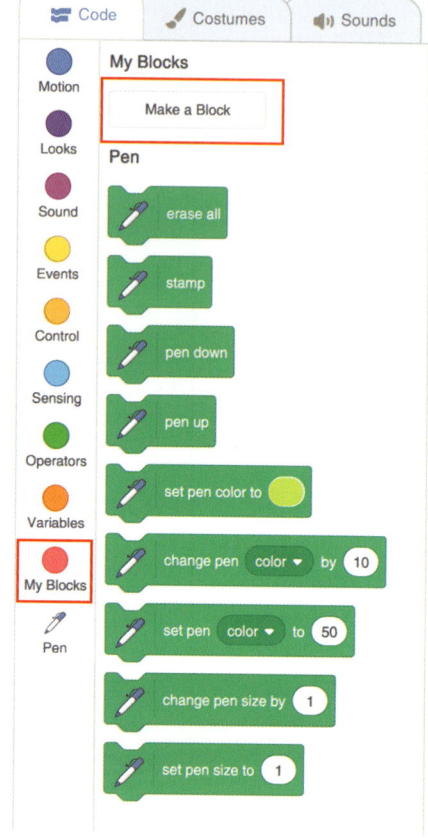

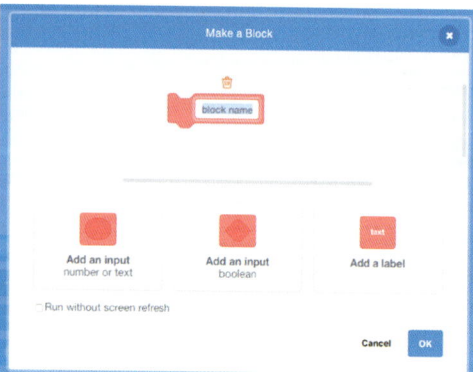

You then give your procedure a sensible name.

This procedure will draw a square, so it is named 'Square'.

Then click 'OK'.

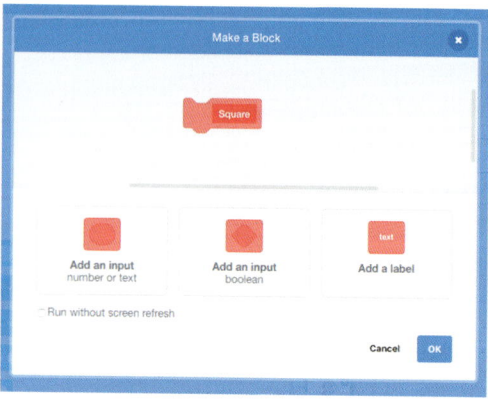

1 Exploring programming

You can then put your code under the new block ('define Square').

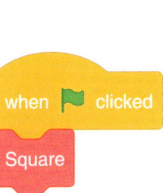
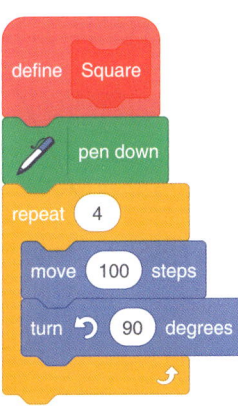

Then tell the algorithm to go to the procedure from the **More Blocks** menu. This is known as 'calling' the procedure.

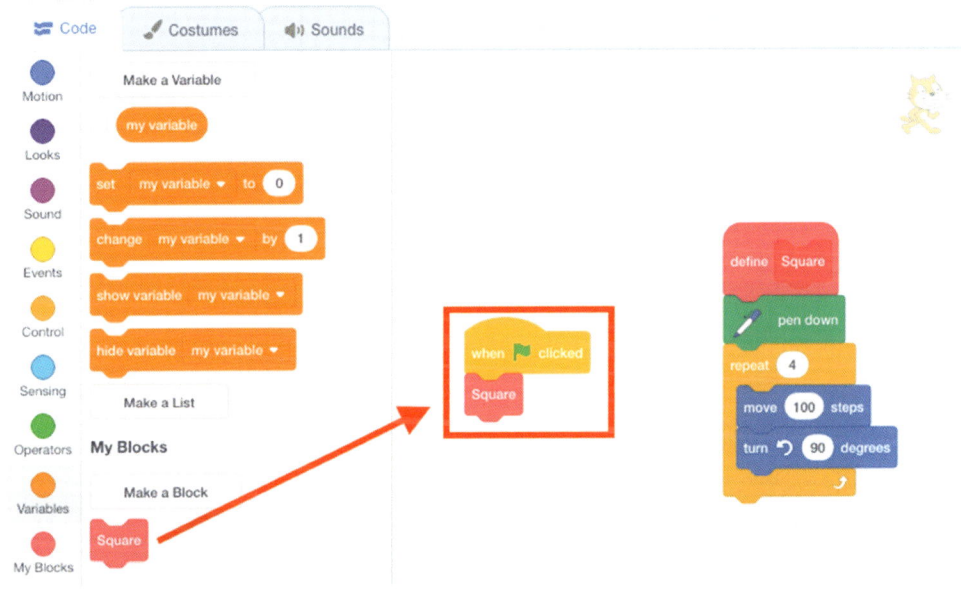

Activity 9.1
Create a procedure to draw a rectangle. Name this procedure 'Rectangle'.

Add code so when the green flag is clicked, the rectangle procedure is run.

Activity 9.2

In the same Scratch program as **Activity 9.1**, create a new procedure to draw a hexagon. Name this procedure 'Hexagon'.

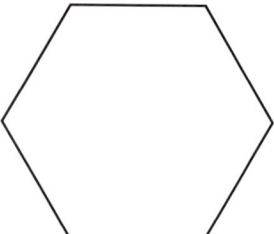

Call the hexagon procedure after the rectangle procedure.

Activity 9.3

You can create this image by calling a rectangle procedure twice and turning 15 degrees in between the procedure calls.

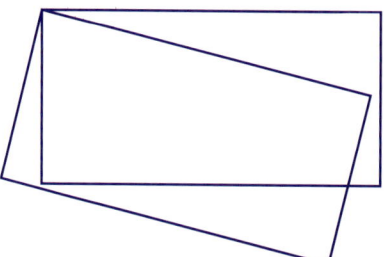

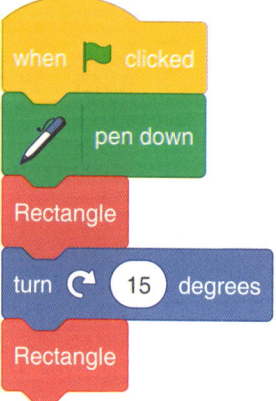
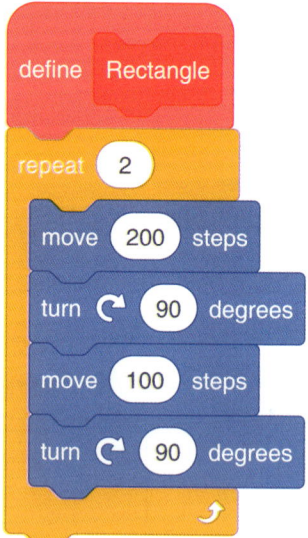

Use your rectangle procedure to draw this shape.

1 Exploring programming

Activity 9.4

Use a repetition block to continually call the rectangle procedure and turn 15 degrees to create this shape.

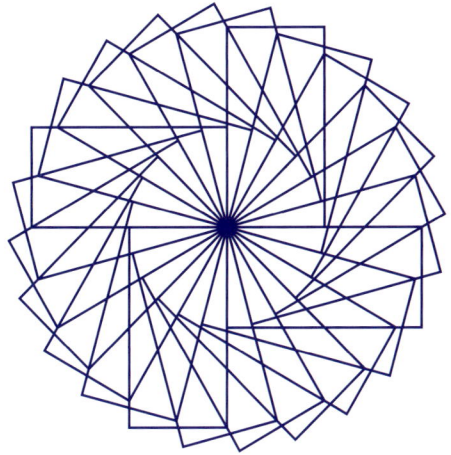

Tip

To complete the circle you need to turn 360 degrees. You are turning 15 degrees each time. The number of repetitions is 360 / 15.

Activity 9.5

This image is made from a repeated hexagon and a straight line.

Use the procedure to draw the hexagon. Call the procedure repeatedly, turning slightly between each repetition to draw the top. Join a straight line to draw the stem.

Skill 10

Using decomposition

Problems can be split down into smaller problems. These can sometimes be split down further into many smaller problems. The smaller a problem is, the easier it might be to solve. The lollipop sign is one large task. It will be easier after you split it down into smaller problems.

Once you've solved the small problems, you can combine them to create a solution to the big problem! This is called decomposition.

You can do this with shapes.

This image is made up of three shapes:

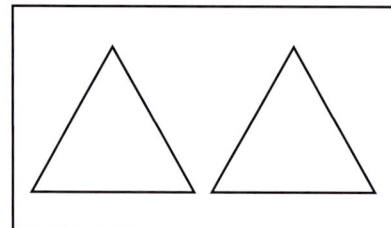

- Rectangle
- Equilateral triangle
- Equilateral triangle

You will need to create a procedure to draw the rectangle.

Both triangles are identical. Only one procedure is needed to draw the triangle. You can then call it twice.

You then need to work out how to get from one place to the next. For example when the rectangle is finished the Sprite will not be where the triangle needs to start.

You need to use [pen up] to stop drawing, then move the Sprite to the new position, for example:

- Pen up.
- Forward 20.
- Turn left 90 degrees.
- Forward 50.
- Turn right 90 degrees.

Tip

Give the procedures appropriate names so you know what they do.

1 Exploring programming

Then call the procedure to draw the first triangle.

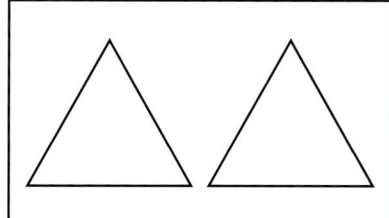

Activity 10.1
Create a program to draw the shape.

Use two procedures.

Activity 10.2
Decompose this image into the two shapes it is made from.

Create a procedure for each shape.

Create a program to draw the image.

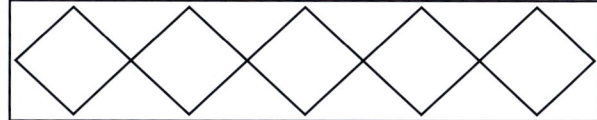

Activity 10.3
Decompose this image into the two shapes it is made from.

Create a procedure for each shape.

Create a program to draw the image below.

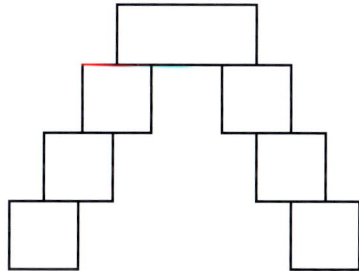

Activity 10.4

Decompose the house into its individual shapes.

Create a procedure for each shape.

Create a program to draw the house.

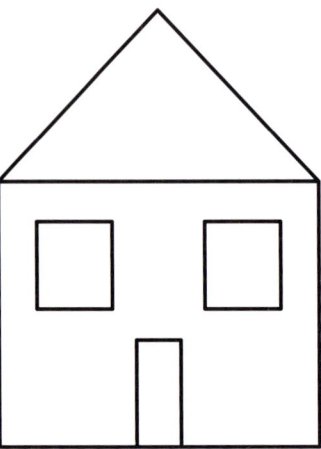

Scenario

Asha's train

Asha has drawn a picture of a train and wants to create a program to draw this train. The shapes do not have to be exactly the same size as those shown; for example the circles might be a bit larger or smaller – that is ok!

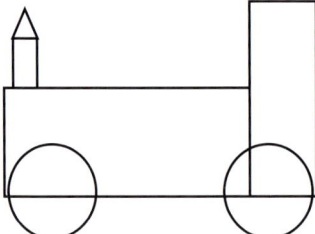

1 Exploring programming

Activity 1
Asha has drawn a flowchart for part of the train.

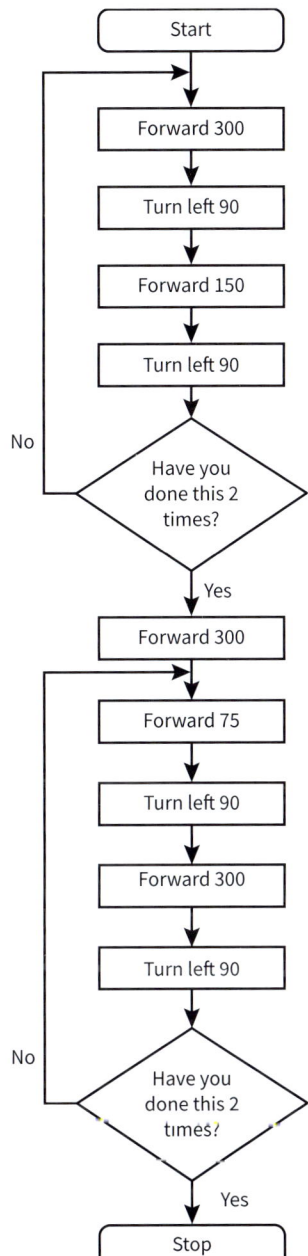

Predict which part(s) of the train the flowchart will create.

Activity 2
Asha was going to create the train in one program but has been told it is better to use decomposition and create procedures.

Decompose the train into its individual shapes.

Activity 3
Create a flowchart for each individual shape you have identified in **Activity 2**.

Activity 4
Create a procedure for each flowchart you produced for **Activity 3**.

Activity 5
Combine the procedures in a program to create the train.

You will need to move the Sprite to its new position after completing one shape, before starting the next.

> **Challenge**
>
> You can change the colour and size of the pen to draw images with different colours and different thicknesses of lines.
>
>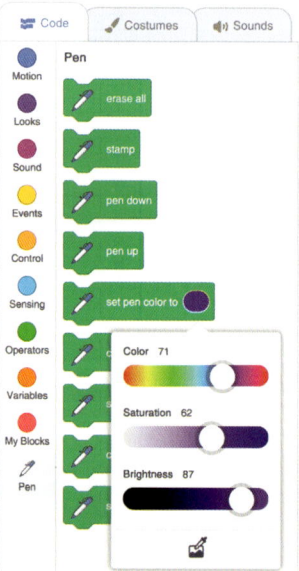
>
> The `set pen color to` block will change the colour of the line. When you click on the coloured box it will give you a number of options to explore.
>
>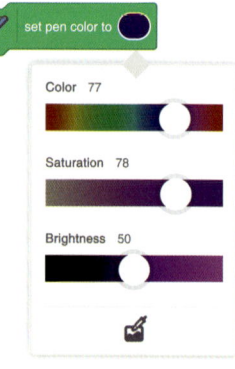

1 Exploring programming

Dragging the Colour bar will allow a change of colour.

Dragging the Saturation bar will make the colour stronger or more transparent.

Dragging the Brightness bar will brighten or dim the colour.

Change the number in the `set pen size to 1` block to change the size of the pen.

The `change pen size by 1` block gives an interesting effect.

Activity 1
Create a program that draws a line, the first half in black, the second half in blue.

Activity 2
Create a program that draws a line that slowly gets darker.

Activity 3
Rewrite your program for **Activity 2** using a repetition statement.

Activity 4
Create a program that draws a line, the first half with pen size 1, the second half with pen size 20.

Create a program that draws one rectangle in red, with a thin line, then a second rectangle in green, with a thick line.

Activity 5
Create a program that has a procedure to draw a shape, for example a hexagon.

Repeatedly call the procedure, turning 15 degrees between each call, alternating the colour and thickness of the line each time.

> **Tip**
> Move forward a small number of steps, then change the shade, then move forward, and so on.

Final project – Shamim's sweet shop

Shamim owns a sweet shop.

She has drawn an image of lollipops that are going to be part of the sign for her shop.

Shamim wants you to write a program to draw her sign.

You will need to use the skills you have learnt in this module to help Shamim by creating a program to draw the sign.

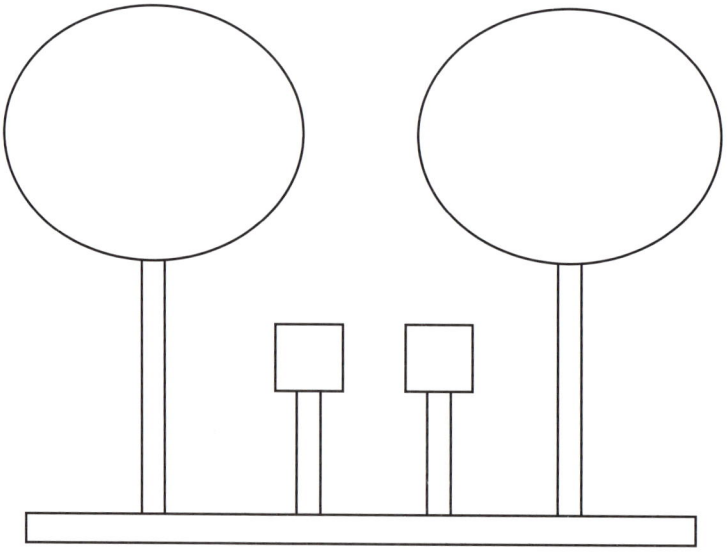

1 Exploring programming

Activity 1
Shamim has planned part of the image using a flowchart.

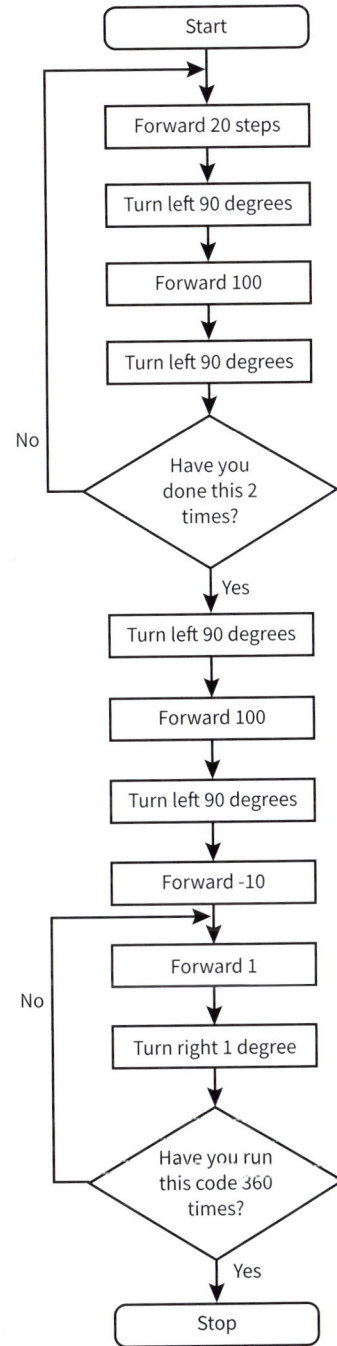

Predict which part(s) of the image the flowchart would produce.

Activity 2
You need to produce the image using procedures.

Decompose the image into its individual shapes.

Activity 3

Create a flowchart for each individual shape you have identified in **Activity 2**.

Activity 4

Create a procedure for each flowchart you identified in **Activity 3**.

Activity 5

Create a program to draw the image using your procedures from **Activity 4**.

You will need to move the Sprite to its new position after completing one shape, before starting the next.

Reflection

1. How can using repetition help to write a program?

___

___

___

___

___

2. What are the benefits of using procedures in a program?

___

___

___

___

___

Exploring the internet 2

	In this module, you will learn how to:	Pass/Merit	Done?
1	Use internet tools to find information	P	
2	Assess the relevance and usefulness of material	P	
3	Store and recover information	P	
4	Copy and paste information from a website	P	
5	Save URLs and objects from a website	M	
6	Use advanced search skills.	M	

In this module you are going to develop skills to help you work towards your final project. You are going to produce a fun guide to give to your friends that will help them do research on the internet. The guide will also include important information about staying safe online.

Before you start on your final project, you will learn how to use the internet to research information and record your findings. You will find out how to use some of the tools available in a web browser. In this module, you will be using, as a web browser, Google Chrome. Then you will complete a report. For this report, you will need to research information and show where you got the information from.

You will also learn how to:
- create folders for bookmarks
- keep yourself safe when working online.

Key words

Online: working on a computer that is connected to the internet.

Webpage: a single page in a website.

Internet: the name given to the network of computers connected across the world.

Website: a collection of webpages.

World Wide Web (WWW): the part of the internet for all of the webpages and websites.

Did you know?

The World Wide Web was invented in 1989 by Sir Tim Berners-Lee. The first website was created in 1990.

Before you start

You should know:

- what copying and pasting information means
- how to use the basic navigation tools in a web browser, such as the 'Forward' and 'Back' buttons
- what a hyperlink is
- how to use keywords to search for information.

Stay safe!

It is really important that you know how to keep yourself safe when you are **online**. You should follow these guidelines so you don't find offensive or illegal information:

- Make sure that you choose your search words carefully. Any misspellings or general search words that don't give enough information, might give you results that are not useful or possibly harmful.
- Look out for any warnings given when opening a **webpage** that it might contain harmful information.
- Remember that not all search results will be reliable. Only click on the links for the results that are well-known and reliable websites.
- Remember that the first results might not always be the best ones. Some companies pay to have their results at the top. You can see which ones these are as they may have 'Ad' or 'Sponsored' next to them.

If you do find a webpage that has harmful information, tell your teacher straight away. You will not be in trouble.

Introduction

The **internet** contains many millions of **websites** made up of many millions of webpages. That's a lot of information! These are found in a part of the internet called the **World Wide Web**. To be able to find the information that you need, you must be able to search the internet in a safe and efficient way. You might also want to keep a record of the searches that you make, and save information or webpages to be used again at a later date.

2 Exploring the internet

Skill 1

Understanding a web address

Every webpage on the internet has a unique web address or **URL**, which can be used to find it. This appears in the address bar of the web browser when you open the webpage. You might have even typed a URL into the address bar to bring up a webpage, if you already know its address.

There are three parts to a URL:

1. It will usually start with 'http' or 'https'. This part is called the protocol, which is the set of rules that governs how data is transmitted for the website.
2. Then you have the part that identifies the website. For example 'www.google'. This part is called the domain name.
3. URLs can end in lots of different ways, depending on the type of website and where in the world it is located. These are called domain extensions. Some common ones are:

   - .com
   - .org
   - .net
   - .de
   - .edu
   - .gov
   - .cn

Activity 1.1

There are many domain extensions, such as '.nz' for New Zealand.

What is the domain extension for your country?

Make a list of any others that you have come across and share the list with a friend. You could make a whole class list.

> **Key word**
>
> **URL:** this stands for Uniform Resource Locator, and is the address of a page or a site on the World Wide Web.

Skill 2

Understanding how a search engine works

If you don't know the URL for a website, or you don't know where to find the information you are looking for, you need a **search engine**. These are fantastic tools. They allow you to search through the huge number of webpages available to find one that you want.

> **Key word**
>
> **Search engine:** a program that is used to search large databases that contain websites from the World Wide Web.

Key words

Address bar: a space in a web browser that shows the address of the webpage being viewed.

Index: a list of all the keywords and webpages that a search engine has visited before.

Algorithm: a list of stages or steps that a program follows in order to solve a problem.

Filter: to remove information that you do not want, or to find information that you do want.

To use a search engine, you type keywords, or a sentence, into the search bar or **address bar** of the browser you have chosen.

Search Google or type URL

Each search engine has something called an **index**. This is a list of all the keywords and webpages that it has visited before, that match these keywords.

The search engine uses a complex **algorithm** to search the index and find all the webpages that match the words typed into the search bar or address bar.

It will then show these results in a list of webpages for you to choose from. It uses another complex algorithm to decide which webpages to display at the top of the list.

There are several different search engines that you can use. Each of them will give you slightly different results. This is because the algorithms that they use will be slightly different.

One search engine that you may use is Google. Another search engine that you could use is Bing.

Some search engines, such as Kiddle, are aimed at young children. You need to make sure that the link that you click is suitable for your age. If you use a search engine like Kiddle, this can help **filter** out the results that might not be suitable for your age.

Activity 2.1

From your web browser open Google by typing it into the address bar.

Now type 'ancient Egyptian pyramids'.

Make a note of the top five search results.

Now open the search engine Bing and do the same thing.

Then open Kiddle and go through the same steps.

2 Exploring the internet

Look at the top five search results in each. How many of them are the same? How many of them are different? Are they all in the same order?

Activity 2.2

Repeat **Activity 2.1** but this time search for 'whales'.

Were your findings for both activities similar or different?

Why were the results similar or different?

Did you know?

Encyclopaedia Britannica was first published in 1768. The last printed version was in 2010. 110 Nobel Prize winners and five US Presidents have written material for it.

Key words

Trusted source: a source that will not damage your computer, will give you accurate information and will not cause you to feel threatened or upset.

Reputation: the opinion people have about you.

Accurate: correct in all details.

Wikipedia: a free, online encyclopaedia that is written collaboratively (together) by many people from around the world.

Skill 3

The reliability of information

You will often use the internet to find out information. This might be for a school project or to learn more about something you are interested in.

One of the most difficult things about using the internet is understanding whether or not the information is reliable. You can do this by getting it from a **trusted source**.

A trusted source is often a well-known company or organisation that has a good **reputation**. It will also be a source where a lot of checking of facts will be carried out before the information is put on the website.

An example of a trusted website could be *Encyclopaedia Britannica*. Before the internet, the *Encyclopaedia Britannica* was available as a series of books. It was a big resource used by many people to research information.

The Britannica company spent many years making sure all the information in their encyclopaedias was correct. The information from these books has now been made available on their website and can be updated easily and quickly. Britannica have a good reputation for **accurate** information and could be used as a trusted source.

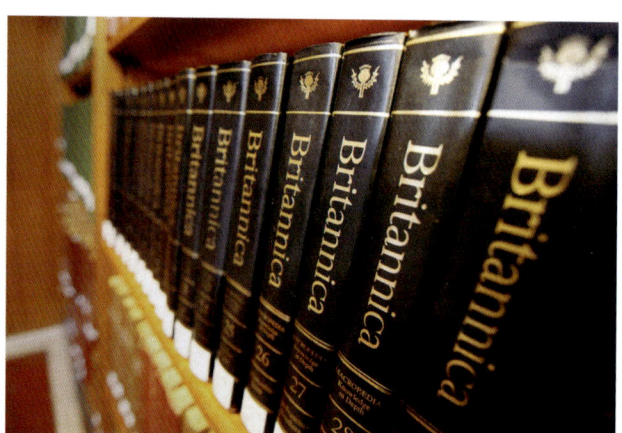

Many people may think that the website **Wikipedia** is a trusted source but you must be careful when using it for finding information. Anyone in the world can change the information that is available on the website, so you might find that information is not very accurate. This means that although a lot of information is available on Wikipedia, it should not be trusted as a source.

To improve the reliability of the information that you find, use more than one source. If you look at the same information across two or more sources, you can see whether they are all giving the same information or if there are differences. If the same information is being given in more than one source, it is more likely that the information is reliable.

Activity 3.1

Type 'The Ice Age' into the search bar.

Look at the top five results.

Look at the source of the information, for example the company or organisation providing it.

Discuss with a partner which result you think would be the most trusted source, and why.

_____
_____
_____
_____

Discuss with a partner which result you think would be the least trusted source, and why.

_____
_____
_____
_____

Activity 3.2

Type 'How big is the biggest dog in the world?' into the search bar.

Look at the top three results and write down how big each one says the biggest dog is.

Do they all say the same? Are they all giving information about the same dog?

_____

_____

Activity 3.3

Type 'How many bees are there left in the world?' into the search bar.

Look at the top three results and write down how many bees each one says are left.

Do they all give the same information?

_____

_____

Key word

Relevant: important to the thing you are looking for.

Skill 4

Filtering information

A search engine will normally give you lots of search results. It is often very difficult to know where to start to find the most **relevant** result.

The most popular results will normally appear at the top of the list as this is where the algorithm is designed to put them.

You might find that the results you get will be from many different countries around the world. You might only want the results from your country.

Many search engines are designed to detect automatically where you are, so you might find that the results you get are from your country. If you wish, you can filter the information to make sure they are.

Once you have typed your keywords or sentence into the search bar, you will see a list of results.

For example, if you use Google Chrome and click on the 'Tools' button you may see a drop-down menu that you can click called 'Any Country'.

2 Exploring the internet

Click the 'Any Country' drop down and you should see a second option of 'Country:' followed by your country. For example, 'Country: India', 'Country: Greece', 'Country: Spain'. If you click the 'Country:' option, it will filter the results to include only those from your country.

If this does not work on your web browser and search engine, experiment by trying it out on another option.

| All | News | Videos | Images | Maps | More | | Settings | Tools |

Any country ▼   Any time ▼   All results ▼

Activity 4.1
Type 'The Ice Age' into the search bar.

Look at the list of results.

Filter the results to include only results from your country.

Did you find the list changed? Did all the results change or just some of them?

_____

_____

Skill 5

Saving a webpage
You might want to save some of the webpages that you find useful so that you can use them again at a later date.

You might also want to keep a list of the webpages you have used for a project to show where you got the information from. There are three ways that you could do this.

Save a link to the webpage
To save a webpage, you can click on the right mouse button in a blank space anywhere on the webpage. You will see a **menu** appear.

You can then click on the 'Save As' option in the menu.

Choose where you want to save the webpage, then click on 'Save'.

If you now go to where you saved the webpage, you should see a link to the webpage.

> **Key word**
>
> **Menu:** a list of items.

Back	Alt+Left Arrow
Forward	Alt+Right Arrow
Reload	Ctrl+R
Save as…	**Ctrl+S**
Print…	**Ctrl+P**
Cast…	
Translate to English	
View page source	Ctrl+U
Inspect	Ctrl+Shift+I

Printing a webpage

You may want to print a webpage so that you can keep a copy of it.

To do this, click on the webpage then click on the right mouse button. A menu will appear.

Click on 'Print' in the menu and this should bring up a preview of the page that you want to print.

Click on 'Print' and the webpage will print.

Back	Alt+Left Arrow
Forward	Alt+Right Arrow
Reload	Ctrl+R
Save as…	Ctrl+S
Print…	**Ctrl+P**
Cast…	
Translate to English	
View page source	Ctrl+U
Inspect	Ctrl+Shift+I

WATCH OUT!

Clicking on 'Print' on a webpage sometimes means that you print lots of pages rather than just the front page you thought you were printing. If you want to print only the page that is showing, then go to your printer settings and choose to print only that page.

2 Exploring the internet

Bookmark the webpage

You could also **bookmark** a webpage so that you can easily visit it again.

To bookmark a webpage, click on the star at the end of the address bar.

Click on 'Done' in the box that appears.

To find a bookmark you have saved, you need to open the bookmark menu. This can normally be found in the top right-hand corner of the webpage but what it looks like will depend on the browser you are using.

Activity 5.1

Create a folder called 'My_favourite_webpages'.

Go to your favourite webpage and create a link to it by saving the webpage in your folder.

Save two other webpages that you like in your folder.

Activity 5.2

Print a copy of your favourite webpage.

Activity 5.3

Go to your favourite webpage and create a bookmark for it.

Close the web browser then open it again and try and find the bookmark you created.

> **Key word**
>
> **Bookmark:** this is a saved shortcut that allows you to go to a specific webpage. This is sometimes called 'Favorites' (the American spelling of 'Favourites').

Skill 6

Saving text from a website

You might want to save text from a website.

You should think carefully before doing this and you should always try to rewrite it in your own words if you can. This is being **academically honest**.

> **Key word**
>
> **Academic honesty:** acknowledging the source of the information.

Key words

Ethical behaviour: showing respect for other people's work, honesty and fairness.

Plagiarism: copying someone else's work without referencing it so it looks like your own.

If you do use text from a website in your own work, you should include a reference that shows where you found it. If you don't do this, you could be accused of **unethical behaviour** or even **plagiarism**.

To save text from a website, highlight the text with your cursor.

Click on the right mouse button and a menu will appear.

Click 'Copy' in the menu.

Open a new document. This could be in Microsoft Word, Wordpad or Notepad.

Click on the right mouse button again and click 'Paste' in the menu.

Activity 6.1

Choose some text from your favourite website and copy and paste it into an appropriate document.

Save the document into a suitable folder.

2 Exploring the internet

Skill 7

Saving a URL

Copy and paste

Copying and pasting the URL for a webpage into a document means that you can save the document and have the addresses saved for later.

To copy the URL for a webpage, highlight the webpage address in the address bar.

Now you have highlighted the URL you can copy it.

To copy the URL, click on the right mouse button and a menu will appear.

Click on 'Copy' in the menu. You have now copied the URL of the page.

Undo	Ctrl+Z
Cut	Ctrl+X
Copy	**Ctrl+C**
Paste	Ctrl+V
Paste and search	
Delete	
Select all	Ctrl+A
Edit search engines...	

To paste the URL in a document, click on a space in the document and click on the right mouse button.

A menu will appear and you need to click on the first 'Paste' option in the menu.

Drag and drop

Another way to save a URL is to drag it into a folder. This creates a copy of the URL in your folder. This is quicker than copying and pasting the URL into a document. However, not all web browsers will let you do this

Tip

To highlight the address, you need to place the cursor at the end of the webpage address and click and hold the left mouse button. Dragging the cursor to the start of the webpage address means you should see that it is now highlighted (this will normally be blue). Alternatively, a single click on the address, anywhere in the address bar, will also select the address.

and you need to have the webpage and the folder open at the same time.

To copy a URL into a folder, you need to click and hold down the left mouse button on either the symbol at the beginning of the address bar in your web browser or the highlighted URL.

You can then drag the symbol or the highlighted URL into a folder you have already created.

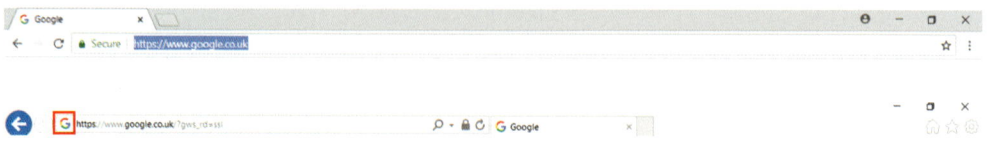

Activity 7.1

Create a document called 'Webpages_I_need'. Go to your favourite webpage and copy the URL for it.

Paste the URL in your document.

Copy and paste two other URLs for webpages in your document.

Activity 7.2

Create a folder called 'URLs_I_need'.

Go to your favourite webpage and drag the URL into this folder.

Do this for two other webpages.

Skill 8

Saving an image from a website

You might want to save an image from a website.

Before you save an image from a website, you need to check whether you have permission to copy it. For some content, only the owner or creator of the image can legally copy and share it with other people. This is called **copyright**.

There are websites that contain copyright-free images that you can save and use in your own work.

As previously discussed, you should include a reference that shows where you found the image.

> **Key word**
>
> **Copyright:** a legal right, given to the owner or creator, which means only they can share the content with other people.

2 Exploring the internet

To save an image from a website, move your cursor to the middle of the image you want to save.

If you click on the right mouse button a menu will appear.

You can then click 'Save image as…' in the menu.

Then you can choose where you want to save the image and click 'Save'.

```
Open image in new tab
Save image as...
Copy image
Copy image address
Search Google for image


Inspect                          Ctrl+Shift+I
```

Activity 8.1
Choose an image on your favourite website and save this image in the folder 'My_favourite_webpages'.

Scenario

Sun facts

You are going to use the internet to research some information about the Sun and create a report of your research.

Activity 1

Open the document 'My_Report.docx' that your teacher will give you.

Change the name of the document so that you can easily identify it as yours, and then save it.

Activity 2

Use the internet to research information about the temperature of the Sun. Copy and paste text from two of the best results from your search to answer each of the questions in the report.

Activity 3

Save an image from one of the webpages you used into your report.

Activity 4

Copy and paste each URL that you use in the report into the table at the end.

Next to each URL, write why you thought that the webpage would be a reliable resource to use.

Activity 5

Create a bookmark for each webpage that you used in your report.

Challenge

Bookmark folders

You might want to have different folders for different bookmarks.

For example, you could keep school webpages in one folder and games in another.

To create a folder for bookmarks, you need to click the star at the end of the address bar. This will open a box called 'Edit bookmark'.

2 Exploring the internet

Click on 'More' and this will open a second box.

Click 'New Folder' and a new folder will appear and you can give the folder a name.

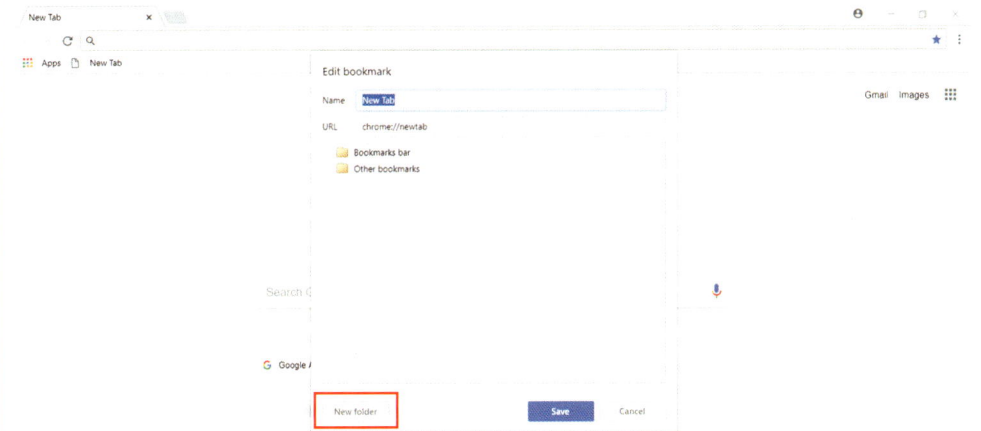

The webpage you bookmarked will now be added to the folder that you created.

To add further bookmarks to the same folder, click on the star and select the correct folder for the bookmark.

Activity 1
Create a folder called 'School'.

Bookmark three webpages you use at school and add them to this folder.

Activity 2
Create a second folder called 'Fun'.

Bookmark two webpages that you like to use for fun and add them to this folder.

Frequently Asked Questions
Something you might have come across on webpages are **Frequently Asked Questions** or **FAQs**.

These are questions that get asked regularly about a particular subject. To save the person who is looking at the website some time, the creator will list these questions and their answers on a section of the website.

This means you don't have to find out the answer yourself and the creator of the website doesn't have to answer the same question over and over again. That would be very time consuming!

> **Key word**
>
> **FAQ:** stands for Frequently Asked Questions. It is normally a list of questions with the answers given underneath.

Activity 3

Write a list of questions you think people frequently ask about our solar system and space.

Compare your list with a classmate's list. Did you write the same questions?

Activity 4

Try to answer your list of questions by searching on the World Wide Web. Add your answers underneath each question.

Final project – How to search on the internet

You are going to write a guide for your friends about how to use the internet properly for researching information and how to be safe online.

Activity 1

Choose suitable software for your guide.

You may choose to do it as a presentation or as a word-processed document.

You could even choose to make a webpage.

Activity 2

Create a guide for your friends to tell them how to use the internet properly and safely.

Make sure that you include how to:

- search for information
- filter the search results for your country only
- choose a reliable source
- save a webpage
- bookmark a webpage
- print a webpage
- be safe online.

Activity 3

Think about whether you want to include a section for FAQs in your guide. Add this to your guide if so.

2 Exploring the internet

Reflection

1 Are all webpages on the internet reliable?

_____

_____

_____

_____

2 Why is it important to make sure that a source is reliable?

_____

_____

_____

_____

_____

_____

_____

Exploring email 3

	In this module, you will learn how to:	Pass/Merit	Done?
1	Create, edit, read and answer emails	P	
2	Add addresses to the email address book	P	
3	Use the address book to send copies (cc), blind carbon copies (bcc) and forward emails	P	
4	View an attachment	P	
5	Add an attachment to an email	M	
6	Use email folders.	M	

In this module, you are going to develop skills to help you work towards your final project. This project will be working with a group of friends to create the front cover for a book called *Adventures on Venus* starring Shaleem the Griffin and Saskia the Dragon. You will send this front cover to each other as an attachment using email.

You will also learn how to:

- create sub-folders
- create groups.

3 Exploring email

Before you start

You should:

- have had experience of using an email account, for example Gmail
- know how to log into your email account
- know how to open, read and **compose** emails
- know how to add an address to an email, and send a copy of an email to a second address.

> **Stay safe!**
>
> It is very important to stay safe when using email. Anyone can send emails to any email address, all they need to know is the address. This is why it is important <u>not</u> to tell anyone your email address unless you know them. It is always best to check with an adult first, like a parent, guardian or teacher.

Introduction

Email is one of the ways to send electronic messages over the internet. In this module you will be using the email account given to you by your school to send and receive emails.

There are two main types of email: **webmail** and **ISP-hosted mail**.

1. *Webmail:* Webmail is an email system that allows you to access your email account via a **web browser** on an internet connected device. Gmail is an example of this. Emails are **hosted** on a **server** and you use a web browser to access them. You can access emails from any browser, anywhere in the world as long as you have the login details.
2. *ISP hosted mail:* ISP stands for Internet Service Provider. They can provide you with an email address.

When you log on to either your webmail or your ISP-provided mail you will be accessing your **mailbox**. This will have all your new and old emails in it.

If you use webmail, then you must be **online**. If you send an email it will instantly be transferred to the server and onwards to its destination.

Key words

Compose: to write, or create a new item, for example to write a new email.

Webmail: you log into your email account using a web browser. You can access this from anywhere.

ISP-hosted mail: you download emails onto your computer using software, for example, Microsoft Outlook.

ISP: Internet Service Provider. The company that provides your internet connection.

Web browser: a piece of software that lets you view websites, for example Internet Explorer, Google Chrome.

Key words

Host: a server that stores your emails. You have to access this server to read or send an email.

Server: a computer that stores files, for example websites, to be accessed by other computers over the internet.

Mailbox: the place where your emails (new and old) are stored.

Online: this is when you are connected to the email server.

Offline: this is when you are not connected. (You can still access old emails already stored on your computer but new emails will not be sent or received.)

If you use ISP-hosted mail you do not have to be online. You can open your account **offline**, to read all your old emails. It won't **download** any new ones until you go online. You can also write new emails offline. They will go automatically into your outbox **folder**. As soon as you go online, the mailbox will send the emails onwards.

If you receive an email and you don't recognise who it is from, do not open it. Either delete it, or check with an adult first.

If you open an email and it has a **hyperlink** in it, do not click it unless you are completely sure it is safe. It is always best to check with an adult first. A hyperlink could take you to a fake website, or it could download some **malware** onto your computer, like a **virus**. Viruses can damage the data on your computer.

Always check carefully who you are sending your email to. Make sure you check the spelling of the email address, because if just one letter is different, then the email might go to someone else.

Finally, never give anyone the password to your email account. You never know what they will get up to!

3 Exploring email

Skill 1

Composing, editing, reading and responding to emails

Composing an email

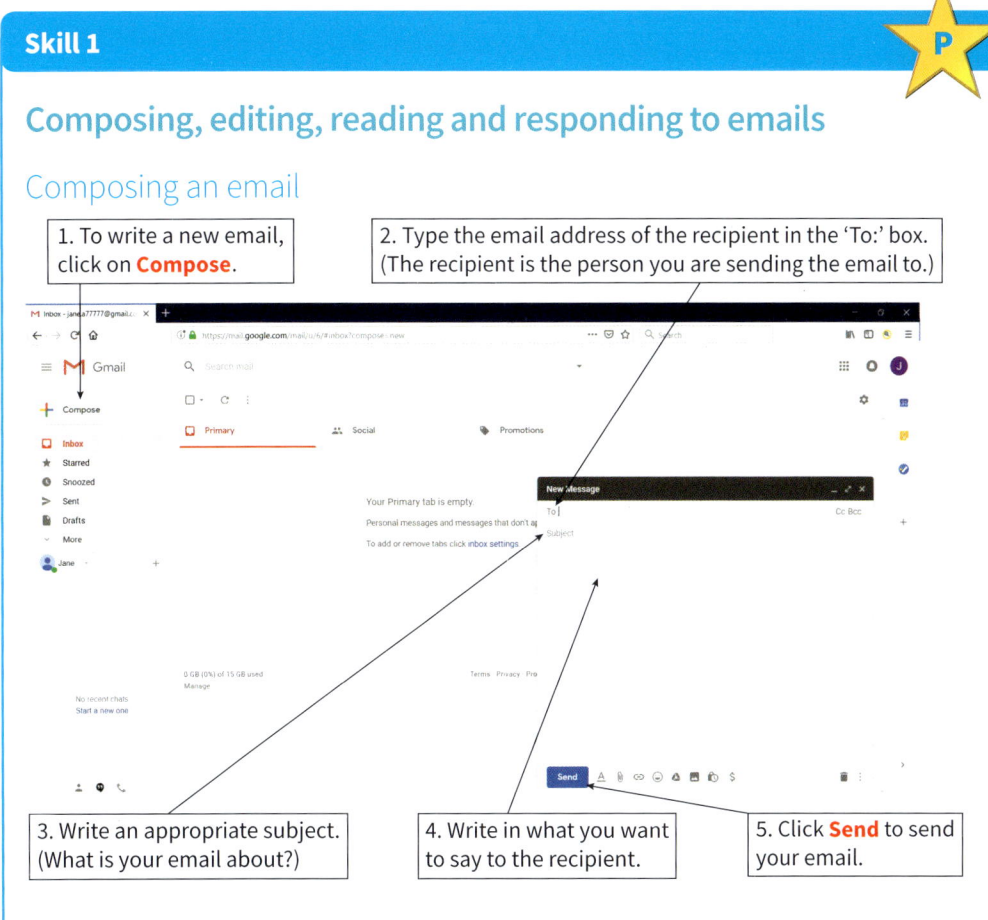

1. To write a new email, click on **Compose**.
2. Type the email address of the recipient in the 'To:' box. (The recipient is the person you are sending the email to.)
3. Write an appropriate subject. (What is your email about?)
4. Write in what you want to say to the recipient.
5. Click **Send** to send your email.

Editing a saved email

You might have started writing an email and it has been saved into your Drafts folder.

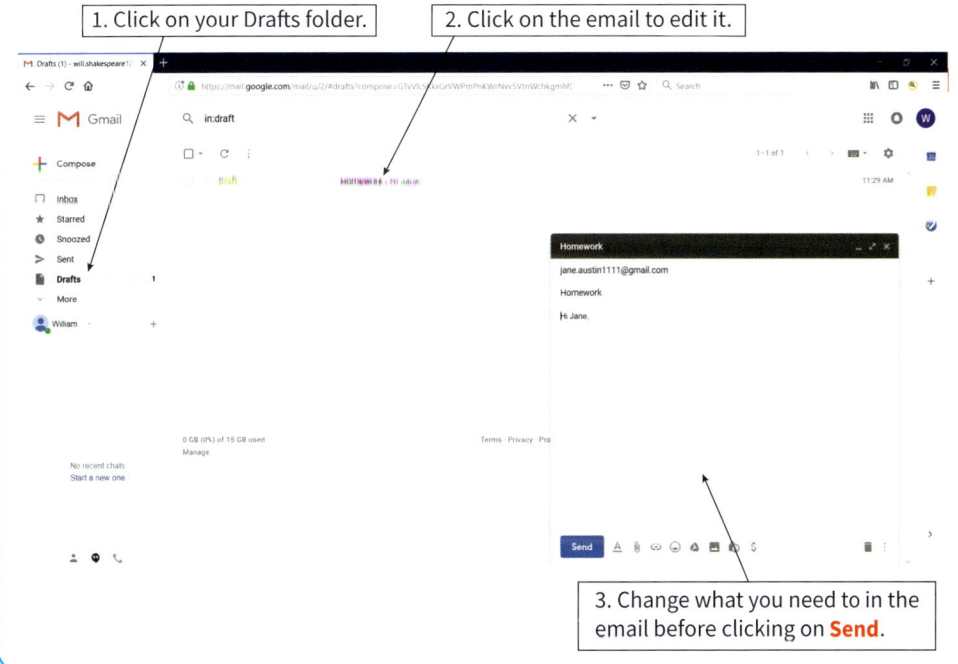

1. Click on your Drafts folder.
2. Click on the email to edit it.
3. Change what you need to in the email before clicking on **Send**.

Key words

Download: to copy data from a computer on the internet to your own computer. Downloading an email means receiving an email from a server onto your own computer.

Folder: a named location in your mailbox. You can move emails into different folders to keep them organised.

Hyperlink: a word or image on a website, or email. When you click on it, it takes you to another webpage.

Malware: software that is installed without your knowledge, usually to damage your computer.

Virus: a type of malware: it makes copies of itself and can damage the data on your computer.

Reading an email

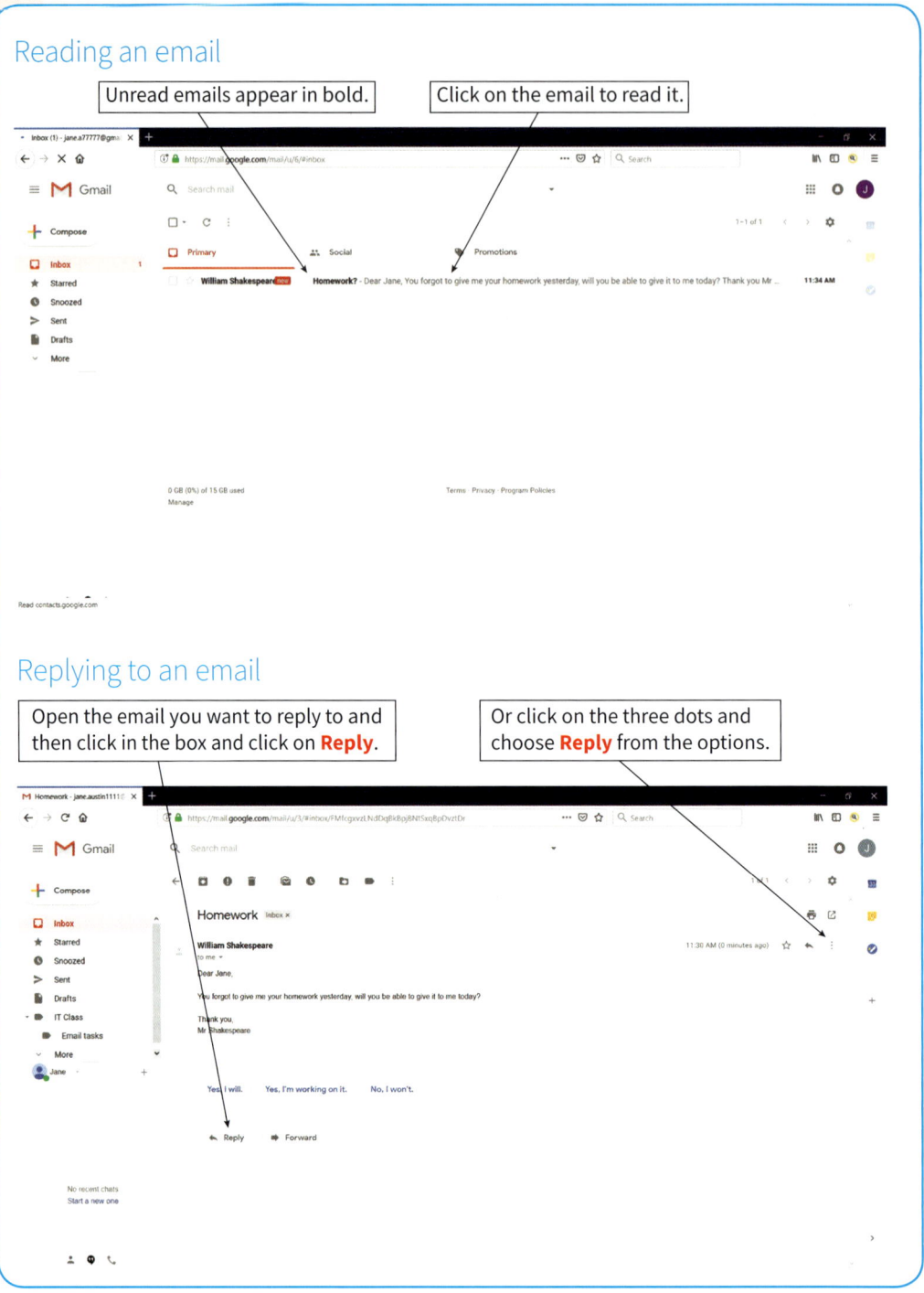

Replying to an email

3 Exploring email

Reply all

Someone might send the same email to you and a number of other people.

You can reply to everyone by clicking on 'Reply all' instead of 'Reply'.

You can also do this using the three dots on the right-hand side.

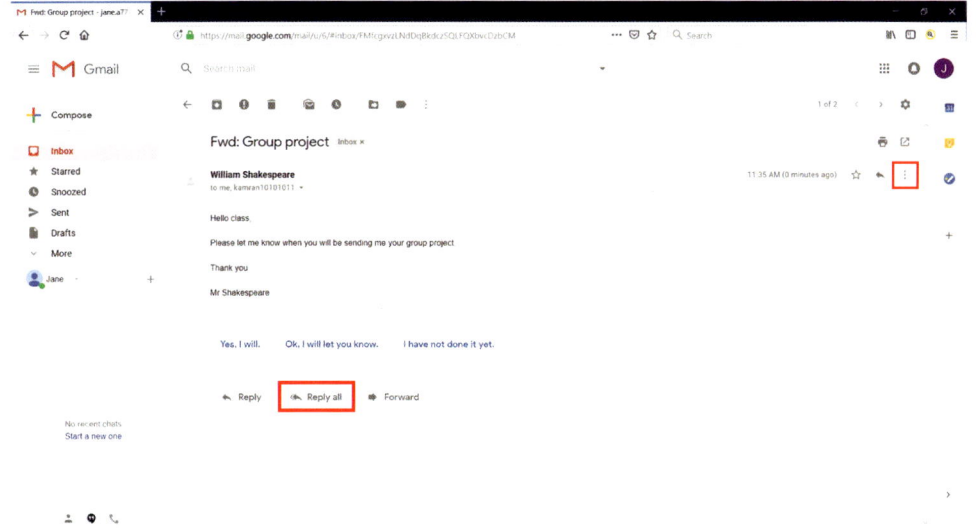

Activity 1.1

Compose a new email to send your favourite joke to one of your friends.

In the email, ask your friend what they think of your joke and ask them to send one back.

Send the email.

Activity 1.2

When you receive a reply, open the email and read what your friend has said, and their joke.

Activity 1.3

Reply to the email from your friend.

Tell them if you found their joke funny, and whether you thought it was funnier than your own joke.

Activity 1.4

Work in a group of three or four people.

Send an email to everyone in your group telling them the name of your favourite musician, or band.

When you receive the emails from each person in your group, search for an interesting fact about each of their choices of musicians or bands.

Reply to your each of your friend's emails, using 'Reply all' so everyone can see the fact you found.

WATCH OUT!

Only use 'Reply all' if you want to send your message to everyone. If you just want to reply to the person who sent you the email, just use 'Reply'.

Stay safe!

Only search for appropriate topics on the internet, and if you see anything you are unsure of tell your teacher.

Tip

Remember to think about the person you are writing to. If you are writing an email to a teacher they might not want it in a large range of font styles, sizes and colours.

Skill 2

Text tools

Formatting

You can format the text in your emails in the same way as when you are using a word processor.

You highlight the text you want to change, then choose from the options shown.

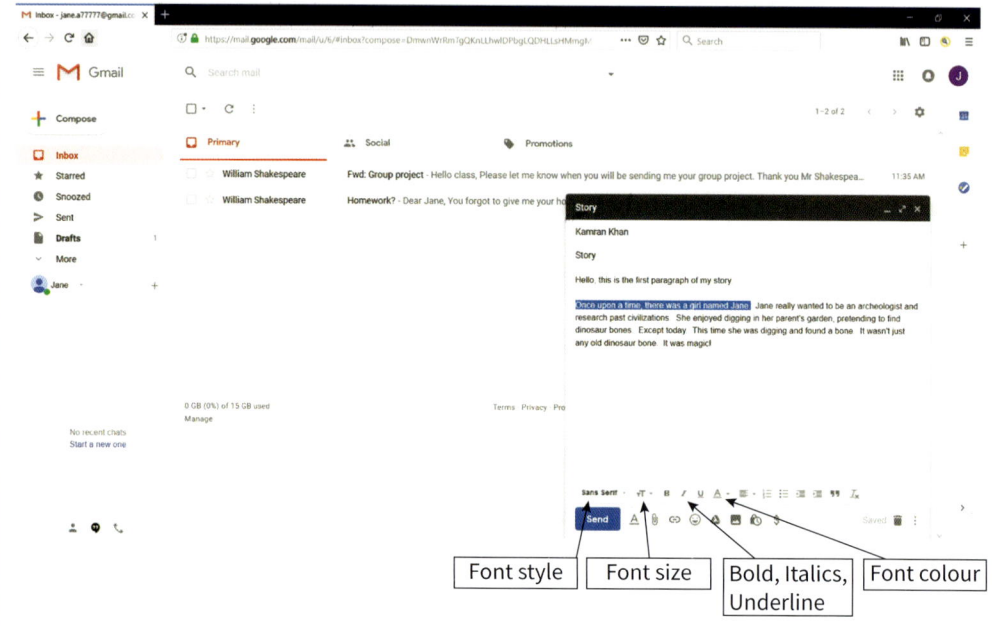

Font style | Font size | Bold, Italics, Underline | Font colour

Spell checker

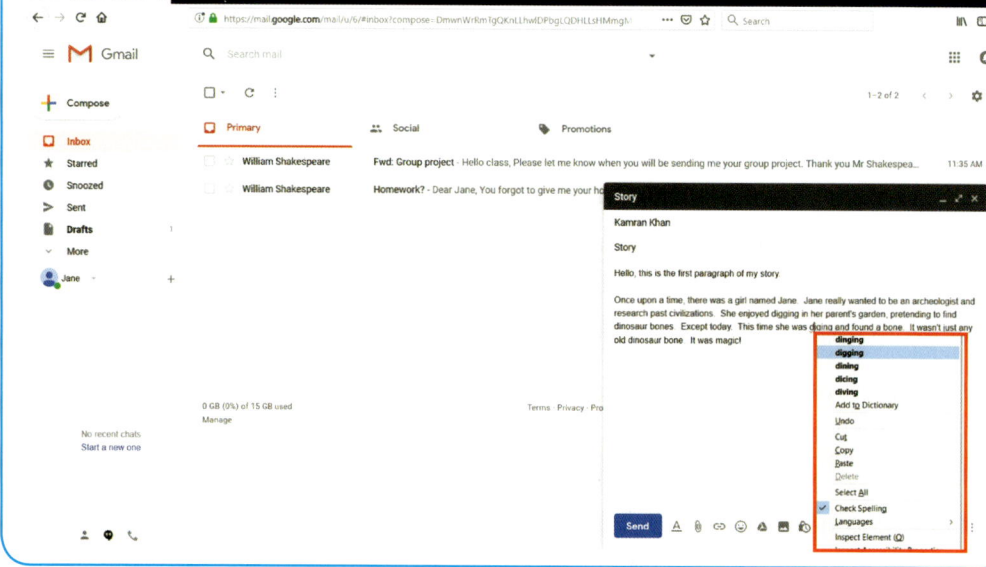

3 Exploring email

You can use the automatic spell checker to check the spelling in your email. Right-click in your email text and make sure 'Check Spelling' is ticked. (If it isn't, click it!)

As you type, any spelling mistakes will be underlined in red.

Right-click on the words underlined to look for the correct spelling.

Copy and paste

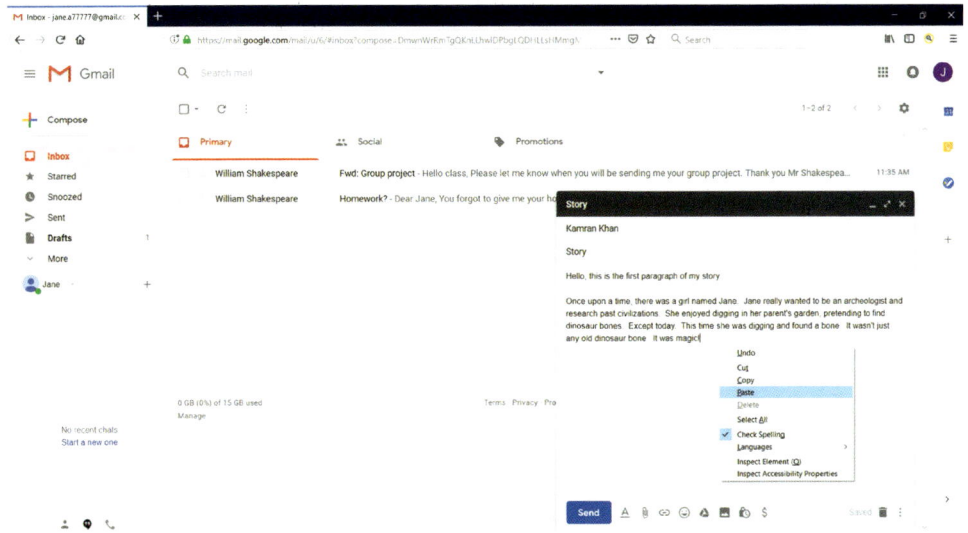

You can copy text from another document into an email to send it to someone.

Copy the text as you usually would in the other document.

Right-click in your email and click on 'Paste'.

Activity 2.1
Shaleem the Griffin and Saskia the Dragon met while at school.

69

On a word processor (for example, in Microsoft Word), write the first paragraph of a story about how Saskia and Shaleem met.

Activity 2.2

Create a new email to your teacher.

Write a message to your teacher, telling them that you are including the first paragraph of the story you have written.

Activity 2.3

Copy and paste the story into the email.

Activity 2.4

Check for any spelling mistakes in your email.

If there are any words underlined in red, right-click on them to see if there are alternatives.

When you are sure there are no spelling errors, send the email to your teacher.

Skill 3

Adding addresses to the address book

Key word

Address book: stores people's names and email addresses so you don't have to remember them each time you want to send them an email.

If you write an email to someone who is not in your **address book**, you can add them.

There are two methods of doing this.

3 Exploring email

Method 1

Open the email in your Drafts folder.

Move your cursor over the person's email address (do not click on it).

Click on the option 'Add to contacts'.

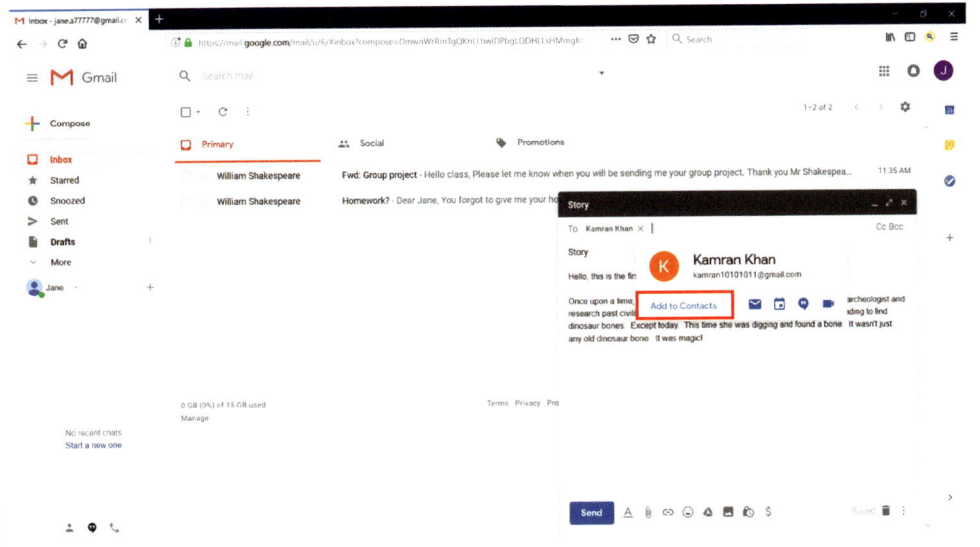

Method 2

You can also add them by clicking on the square of dots on the top right of the screen, and then Contacts.

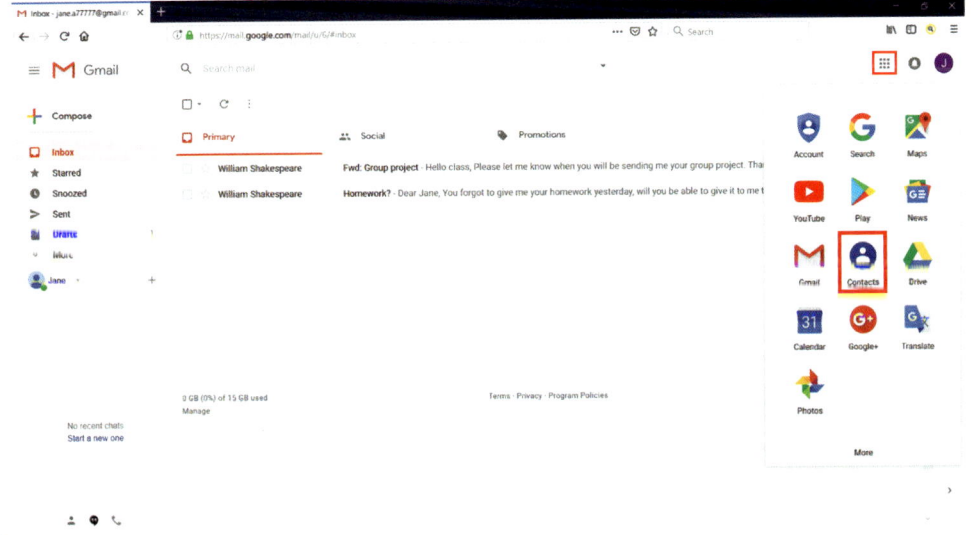

A new window (or tab) will open where you can see all your contacts.

By clicking on the '+' sign, you can add your contact's name and email.

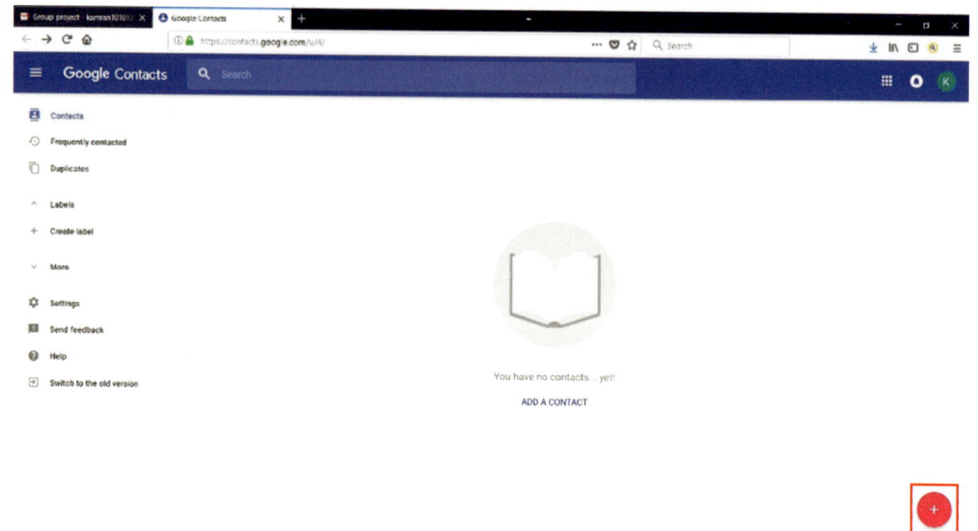

Activity 3.1
Open your current address book by clicking on the '+' sign.

Activity 3.2
Check that all the other people who are in your class are in your address book.

Add any people who are not already in your address book.

Activity 3.3
Your teacher will give you one (or more) email addresses of people you might need to send emails to.

Add these people to your address book.

Skill 4

Address book groups
When you want to send emails to a lot of people, it is quicker to create a **group**.

A group has a name that is easy to understand, for example, 'IT Class'.

The email addresses of the people belonging to that group are all together. In this case, it is all the students in the IT class.

Stay safe!

Only add the email addresses of people who you know in person. If you are not sure, check with your teacher first.

Key words

Group: a name given to a set of email addresses. By using the name, you can send an email to all the addresses at the same time.

Label: the Gmail word for group.

3 Exploring email

When you want to send an email to everyone in the group, you can enter the name of the group instead of everyone's individual email address.

You can follow these steps to add addresses to a group:

1 Open the contacts page for your Gmail account by clicking on the Google Apps button on the top right of the screen.
2 Click on 'Create label'.

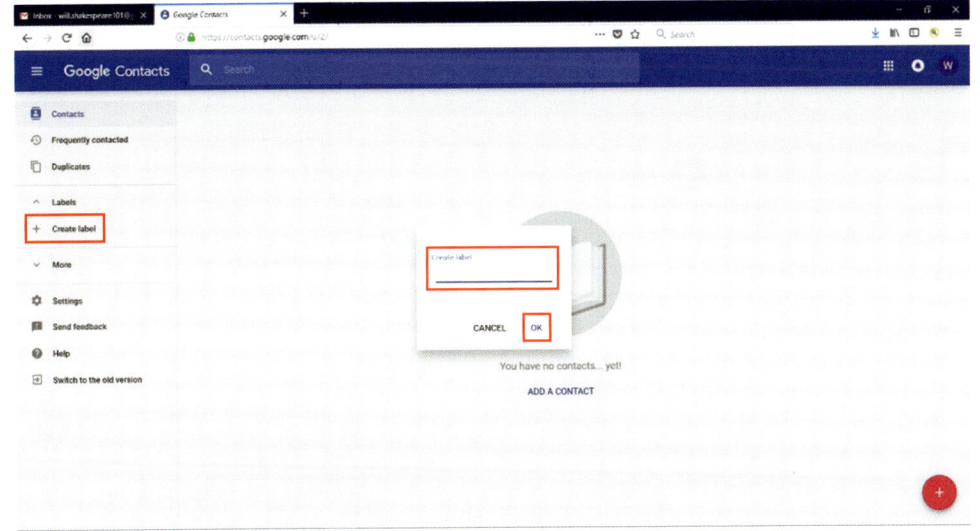

3 Type the name of the group in the space and click on 'OK'.
4 Click on your new label. Then click on the '+'.
5 Enter the contact's details and click on 'Save'.

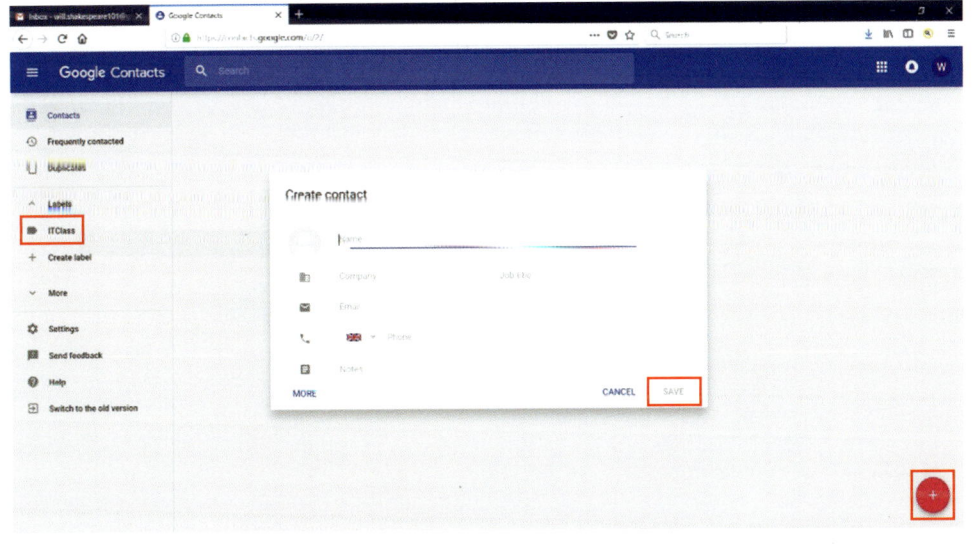

6 Click the '+' each time you want to add more contacts to the group.

73

Stay safe!

Remember to stay safe when using the internet. Only search for appropriate topics, and if you see anything you are unsure of, tell your teacher.

If you already have contacts and want to move them into a group, create the label as before. Select the contact you want to add; this opens them in the screen. Click on the dots and then choose the group you want to add them to.

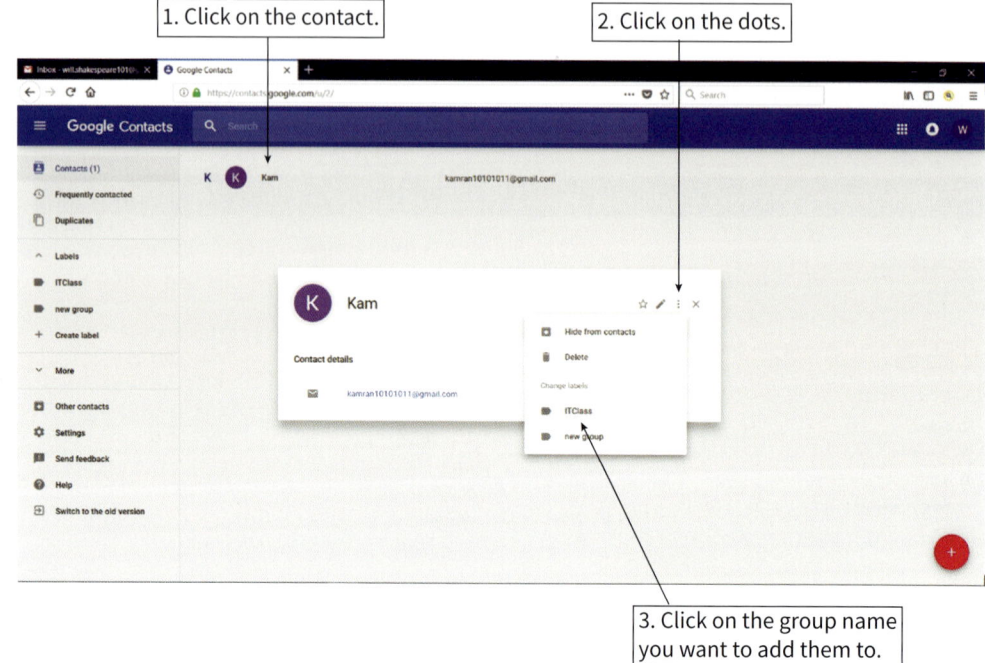

1. Click on the contact.
2. Click on the dots.
3. Click on the group name you want to add them to.

When you want to send an email to the group, type the name of the group in the 'To' box.

The group name will appear with the contacts.

Click on this to insert it.

Tip

If the group name does not come up then:
- check you have spelt it correctly
- check you have created the group.

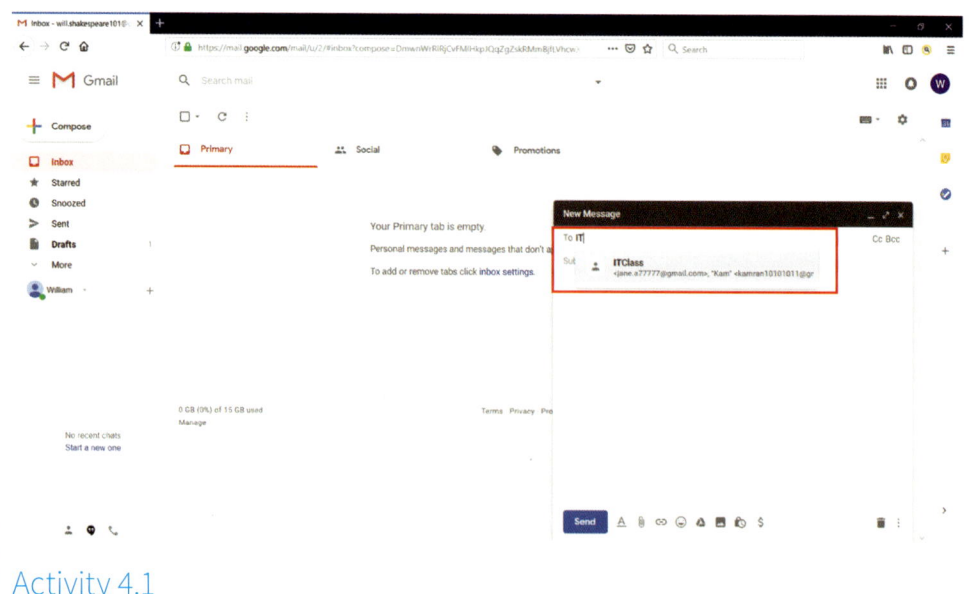

Activity 4.1

Create a new group for your IT class.

3 Exploring email

Activity 4.2
Add all the students in your IT class to your new group.

Activity 4.3
Find an interesting fact about computers on the internet.

Send an email to your IT class group with the interesting fact.

Skill 5

Cc, Bcc and forward emails

'Cc' stands for carbon copy. You can send an email to one person, and Cc in a second person.

The second person gets the email but knows it is probably just for their interest. This is known as 'copying someone in'. For example you can copy in the other members of your group when you are emailing your group project to your teacher.

'Bcc' stands for **blind carbon copy**. You can send an email to one person, and Bcc in a second person. The second person gets the email, but the first person does not know they have received a copy.

You can add a Cc or Bcc recipient by starting a new email and clicking Cc and/or Bcc.

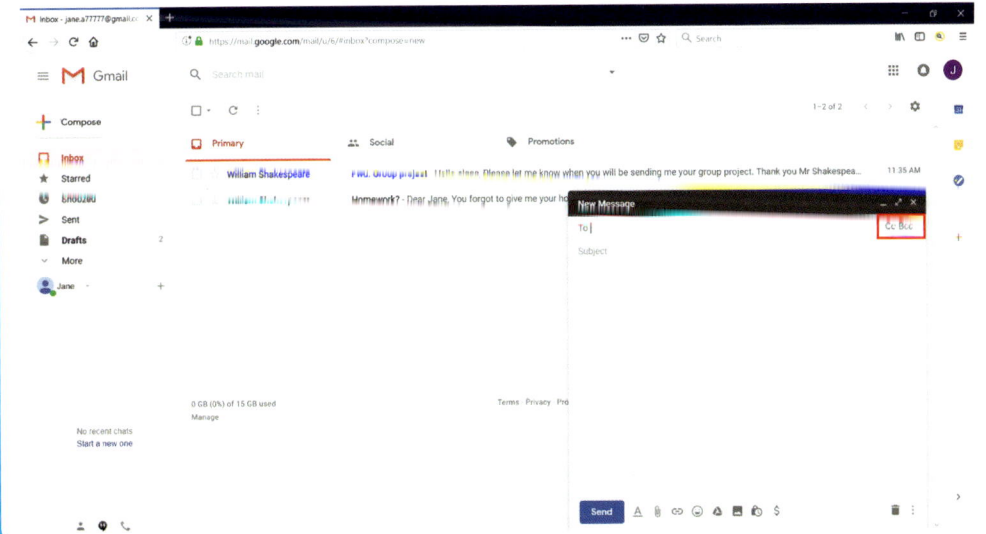

Did you know?
Before email, copies were made using carbon copy paper. When you write on the top sheet, it appears on the one underneath as well. This is how Cc got its name.

Key word
Blind carbon copy (Bcc): a copy of the email is sent to the person who is Bcc'd. The other people who receive the email will not know that the Bcc person has been included.

> **WATCH OUT!**
>
> It is not polite to forward emails you have received from other people without their permission. The content might have been private and they may not have wanted to share it with lots of people.

You can enter the recipient's email address in the Cc and/or Bcc box.

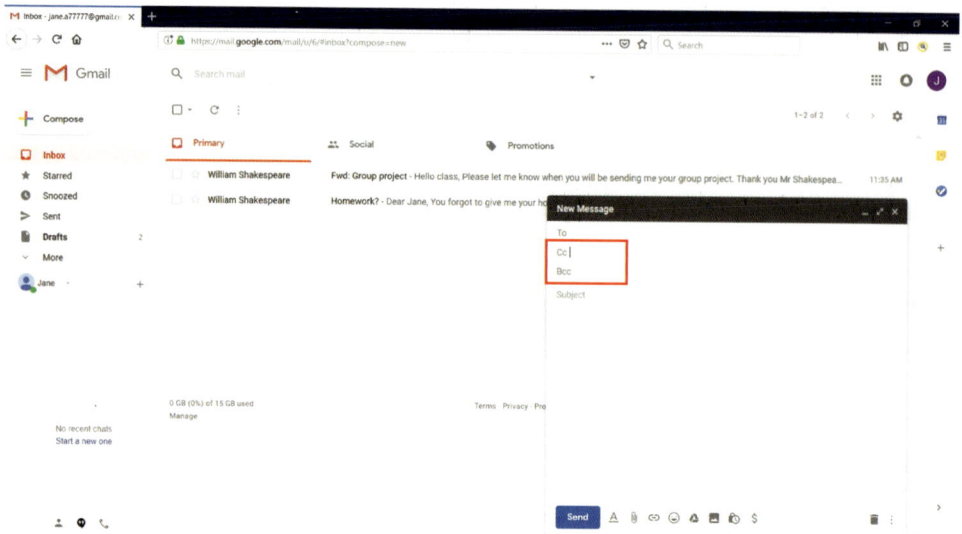

If you start typing the name, email address or group, matching recipients will appear from your address book.

After you receive an email, you can forward it to another person (or several people).

You can add your own message to the top of the email. The previous message will also be included.

You can click on 'Forward' instead of 'Reply', or choose it from the drop-down menu.

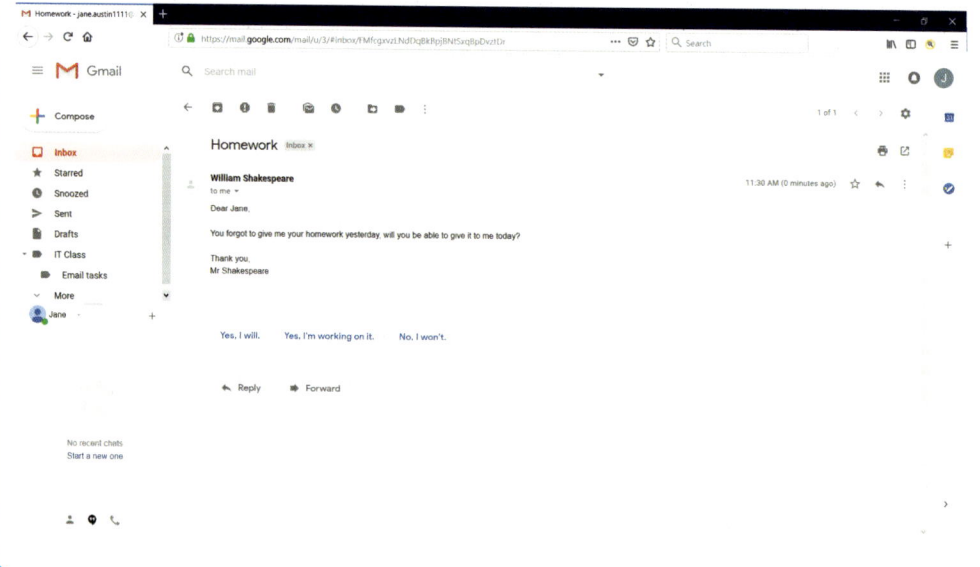

3 Exploring email

Activity 5.1
Find the email containing the joke that you received from your friend as part of **Activity 1.2** in **Skill 1**.

Forward this email to your teacher, telling them why you think it was funny.

Send a copy of the email to the friend who sent you the joke.

Activity 5.2
Add a second paragraph to your story about Shaleem the Griffin and Saskia the Dragon from **Activity 2.1** in **Skill 2**.

Send this to a friend.

Send a Cc to a second friend.

Send a Bcc to your teacher.

> **Did you know?**
>
> An email thread is all the emails, replies and so on that follow on from the one email. For example, you email your friend, they reply, you reply, and so on. If you don't want to see these anymore, then you need to delete all the emails on this thread.

Skill 6

Opening an attachment

An **attachment** is a file that is sent with an email. This could be an image, a word-processed document, or perhaps a video.

When you receive an email with an attachment, the attachment appears below the message subject line.

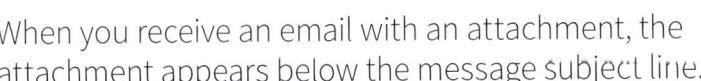

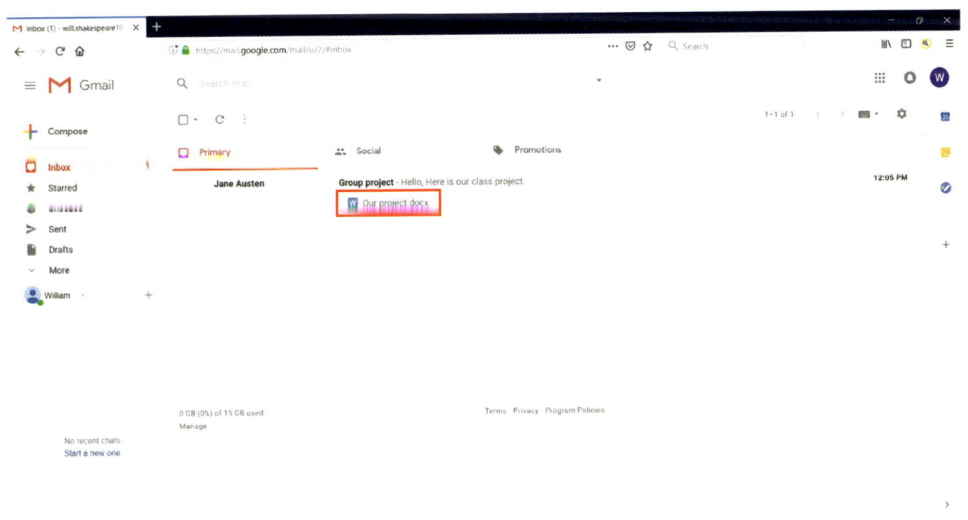

> **Key word**
>
> **Attachment:** a document, or file, that is sent in an email.

When you open the email, the attachment appears at the bottom of the message.

Stay safe!

You should never open an attachment from someone you don't know!

Files could have viruses built into them that can damage not only the computer you are working on but also any computers that may be linked (networked together).

If you are not sure, always ask a teacher before opening an attachment.

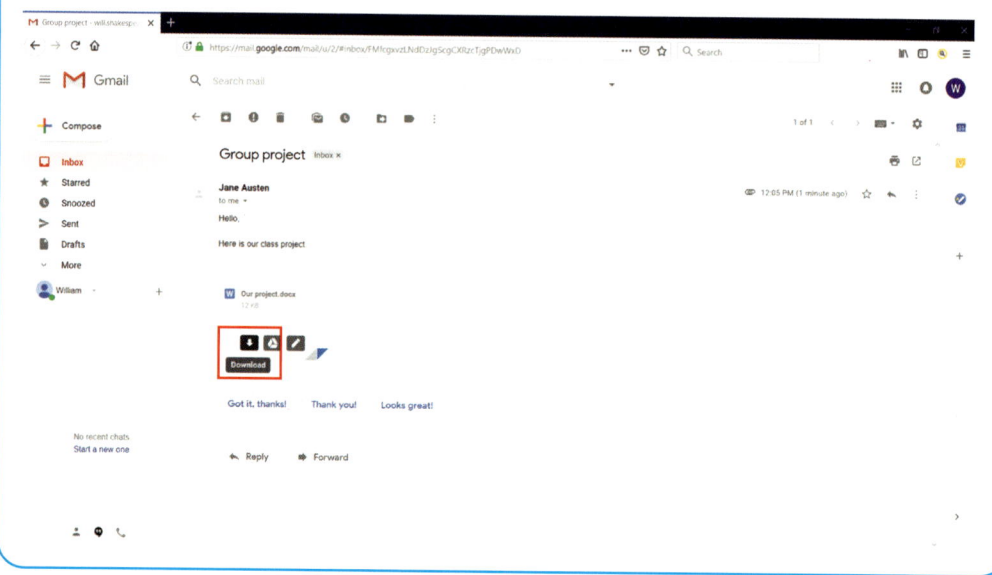

You can click on it to view it on screen.

You can download it by hovering until the download option appears, then clicking on 'Download'.

3 Exploring email

Activity 6.1
Your teacher will send you an email with an image attached. Carefully check that the email is from your teacher.

Open the email and download the image.

Skill 7

Adding an attachment to an email
You can add an attachment to an email and send it to one, or more, people.

To add a file, you need to create an email and then click on the paperclip symbol.

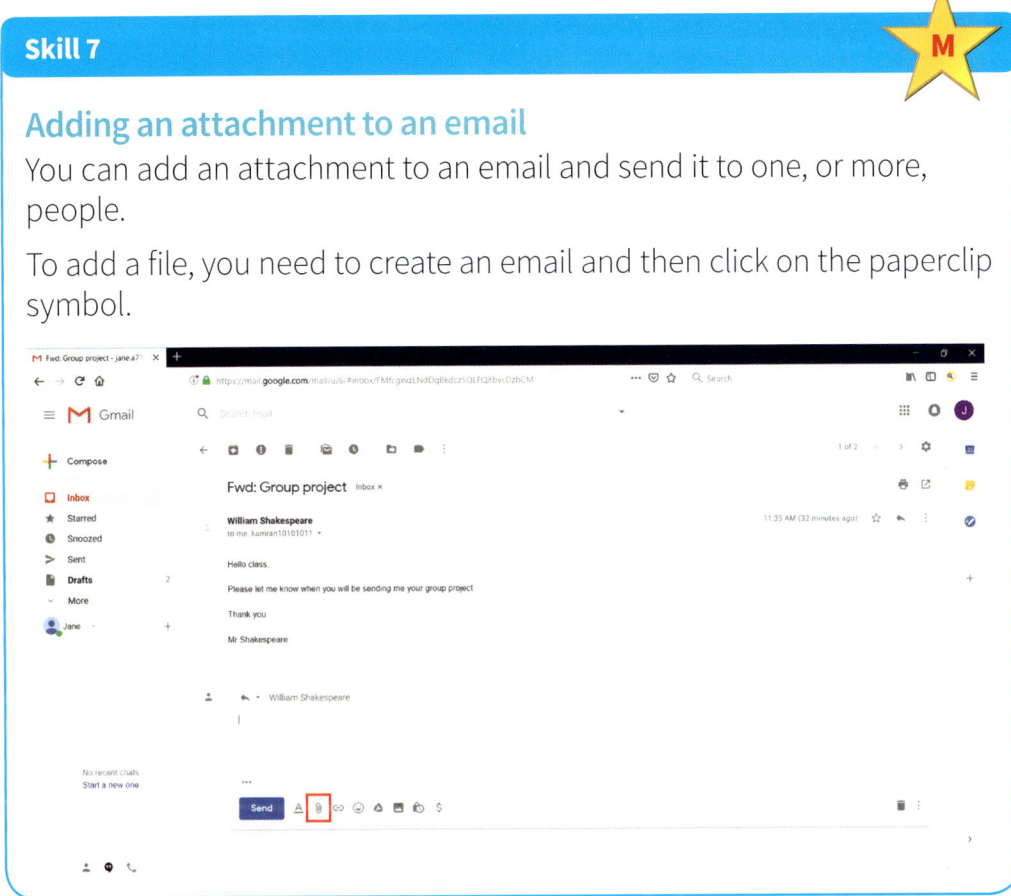

Did you know?
Email systems might have a maximum file size that you can send. In Gmail the maximum file size is 25MB.

You can then choose the file you want to attach.

Find your file by clicking on the folder on the left where it is saved.

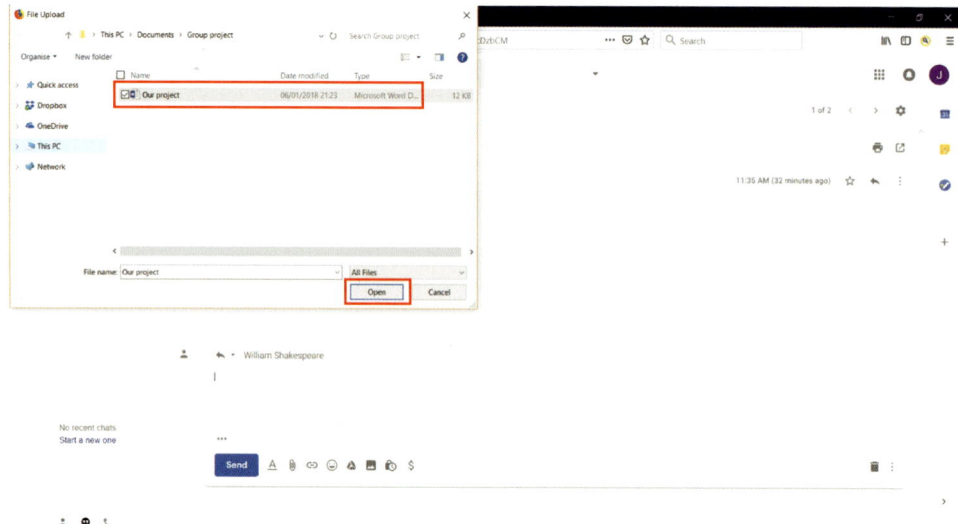

You then need to click on 'Open'.

Activity 7.1

Create an email and attach an image you have drawn on the computer, for example, from the Exploring images module.

Send the email to your teacher with an appropriate message telling them that you have sent them your work.

Activity 7.2

Create an email and attach a word-processed document you have created, for example, from the Exploring documents module.

Send the email to your teacher with an appropriate message telling them that you have sent them your work.

Activity 7.3

Create an email and attach a spreadsheet you have created, for example, from the Exploring spreadsheets module.

Send the email to your teacher with an appropriate message telling them that you have sent them your work.

3 Exploring email

Skill 8

Managing email folders

You can set up folders in your email account in the same way you set up folders to save documents in your computer.

Folders help you organise your emails so they are easier to find when you need them.

To create a new folder, you need to click on 'Create new label'.

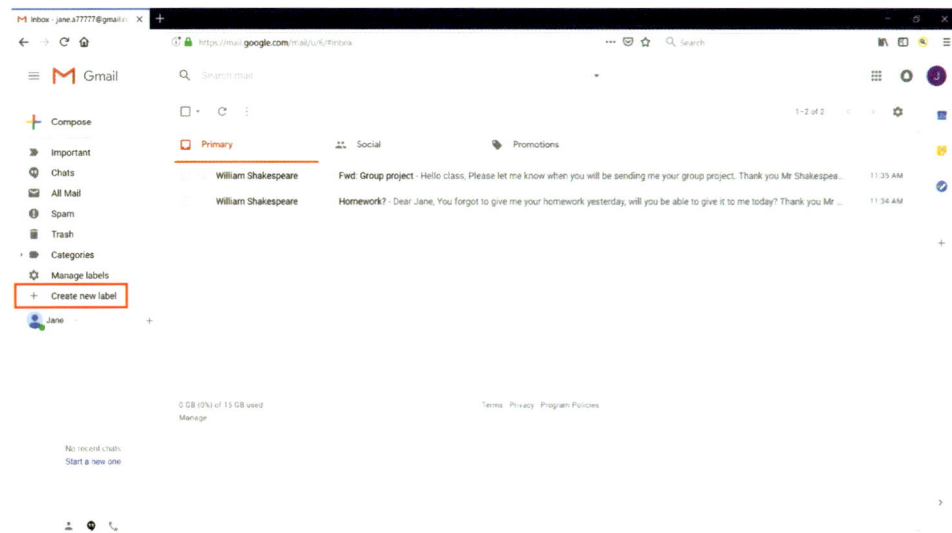

You then need to type in a useful name for your folder, for example, 'IT Class'. This can be used to store emails from your IT class.

Then click on 'Create'.

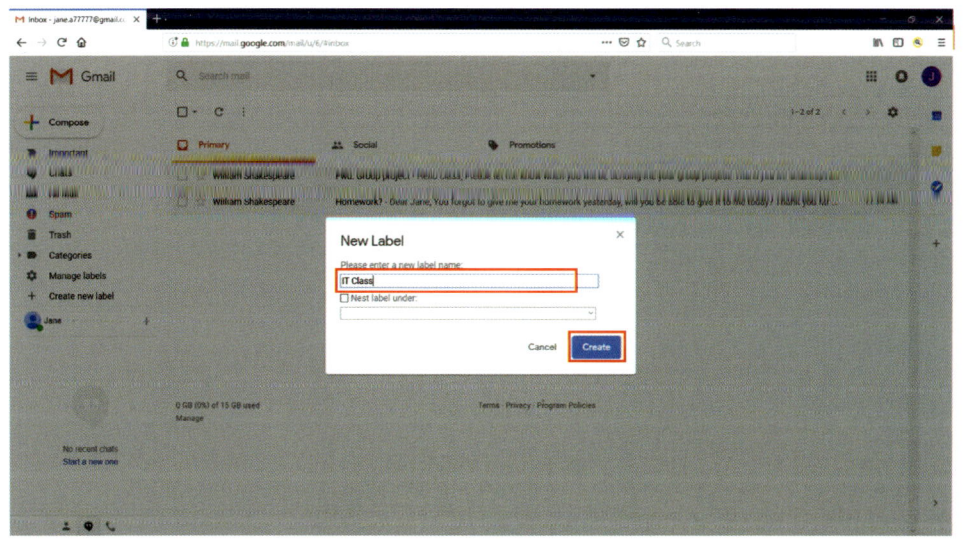

There are two methods of moving the email:

Method 1

To move an email into a folder, tick the box on the left of the email and then drag it into the folder in the menu.

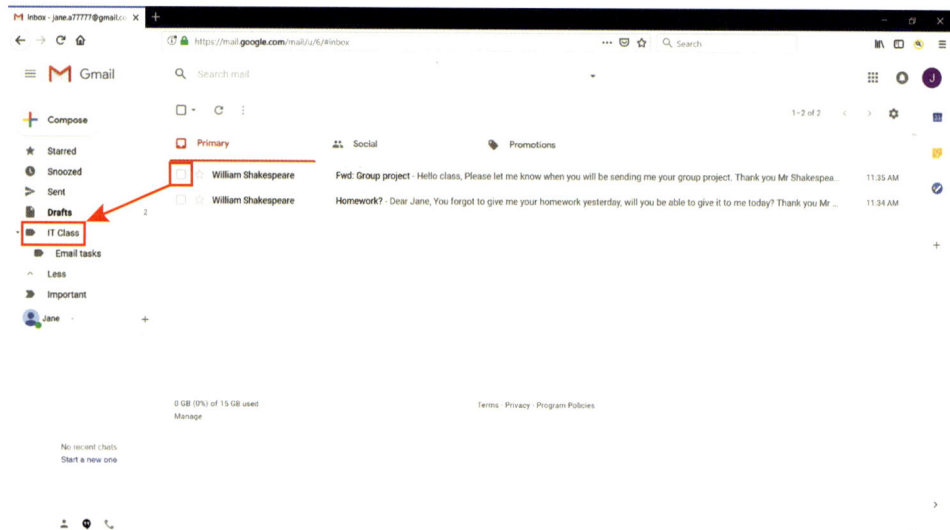

Method 2

Tick the box to the left of the email.

Click on the folder button 'Move to'.

Click on the folder you want to move the email to.

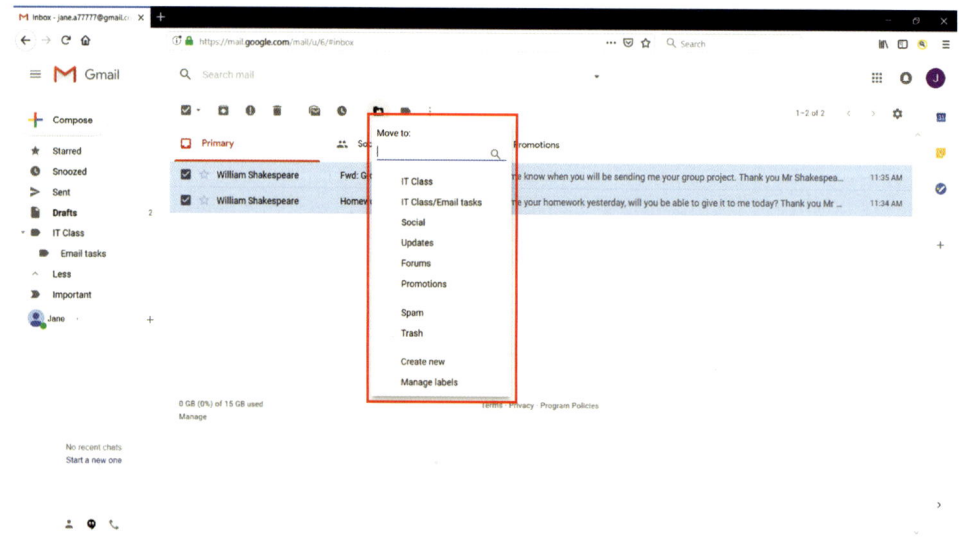

To view the emails in a folder, click on the folder and the emails will be shown.

3 Exploring email

Activity 8.1
Set up a folder for the emails from your IT class.

Activity 8.2
Move all emails that are related to your IT class into this folder.

Activity 8.3
Create a folder for each additional class, or subject, that you might need to use email for.

Move any emails from these classes into the correct folder.

Activity 8.4
Create a 'Social' folder for non-school related emails, for example, from your friends.

Move any emails that are social into the correct folder.

Scenario

Fact finding

Your teacher has a number of questions that they will send you as a document by email. You will need to find the answers to these questions and then send the document back to your teacher with your answers completed.

Activity 1
Create a new folder to store the emails about this activity. Make sure it has a useful name.

Activity 2
You will receive an email from your teacher with an attachment.

Move the email to your new folder.

Stay safe!
Remember to stay safe when using the internet. Only search for appropriate topics, and if you see anything you are unsure of tell your teacher.

Key word

URL: stands for Uniform Resource Locator. It is the name of a website, for example www.google.com.

Activity 3

Download the attachment and open the document. There will be a number of questions that your teacher wants you to find the answer to.

Use the internet (or your own knowledge) to find answers to the questions.

Write your answer to each question in the document. If you used the internet to help you, copy and paste the **URL** of the website you used.

Save the completed document.

Activity 4

You need to compare your answers with a friend's answers.

Email your completed document as an attachment to one friend.

Send a Bcc to your teacher, so they know who you have sent it to.

Activity 5

When you receive your friend's answers, compare them with yours. Are yours correct? If you can't decide, ask your teacher to help. Change any that you need to.

Send your final, completed document back to your teacher. Send a copy to your friend from **Activity 4** so they can see which answers you changed.

Challenge

Creating sub-folders

A sub-folder is a folder inside another folder.

For example you could have a folder named 'IT Class', and within it several sub-folders called 'Email Activities' (to store the work for this module), 'Spreadsheets' and 'Images'.

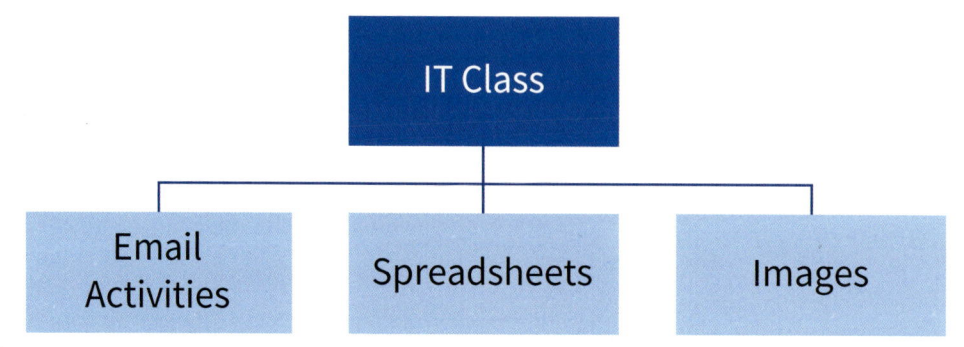

3 Exploring email

Create a folder in the same way as before. When the 'New label' box appears, enter a useful label name and tick the box 'Nest label under'.

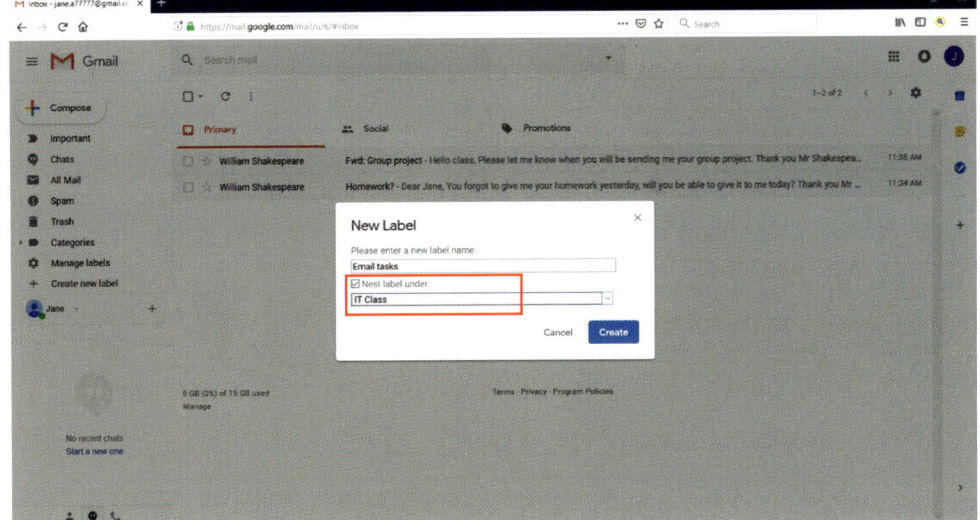

From the drop-down box below, choose which folder you want it to go in. Then click on 'Create'.

Next to your top folder, there will be arrow. Click on this arrow to make the sub-folder appear, or to make it hide.

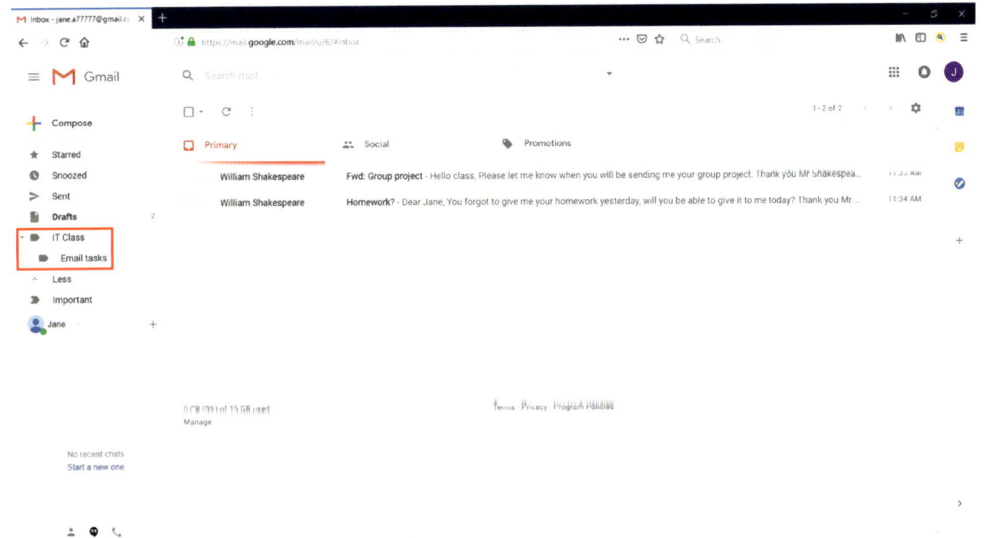

Activity 1

Create these sub-folders within your 'IT Class' folder:

- Next steps email
- Fact finding
- Adventures on Venus

Activity 2

Move all the emails you have sent for this module into the most appropriate folder.

Activity 3

Add any further sub-folders that you think would help you organise your emails.

> **Tip**
>
> If you use an image that someone else has made, make sure you say where you got it from. Copy the web address into the same document.

Final project – *Adventures on Venus*

Shaleem the Griffin and Saskia the Dragon are characters in the book *Adventures on Venus*.

The author needs you and your friends to create an image for the front cover of the book, using email to communicate ideas.

Activity 1

Your teacher will put you into groups of up to four people.

You will need to work with the same group throughout the activity.

Each member of your group needs to be given a number from 1 to 4.

Create a new email group for you and your group members.

Activity 2

Each person needs to create a new email folder for their front cover. Make sure the folder has a useful name.

3 Exploring email

Activity 3

Start a new document in Microsoft Word for your front cover. Add the title only, choose the font style, font size, and so on that you would like.

Save the document.

Activity 4

Write an email to the person who has the number after yours in the group. For example, if you are number 1, send it to person 2. If you are person 4, send it to person 1.

Attach the document with your front cover in to the email.

Send the email.

Activity 5

You will now receive an email from another person in your group.

Move it to the folder for front covers.

Add an image of Shaleem the Griffin to the front cover you were sent. (This can be drawn, or an image taken from somewhere else, for example the internet.)

Save the front cover.

Attach the new front cover and email it to the next person.

Cc it to the person who sent you the email.

Activity 6

You will now receive an email with a front cover that has the book title with Shaleem the Griffin on it. Move it to the front covers folder.

Add Saskia the Dragon to this front cover.

Save the front cover.

Attach this new front cover to an email and send it to the next person.

Activity 7

You will now receive an email with a front cover that has the book title, Shaleem and Saskia on it. Move it to the front covers folder.

Add other details to complete the front cover.

Save the front cover.

Activity 8

Send the final front cover to your teacher. Cc the rest of your group so they can see the final front cover.

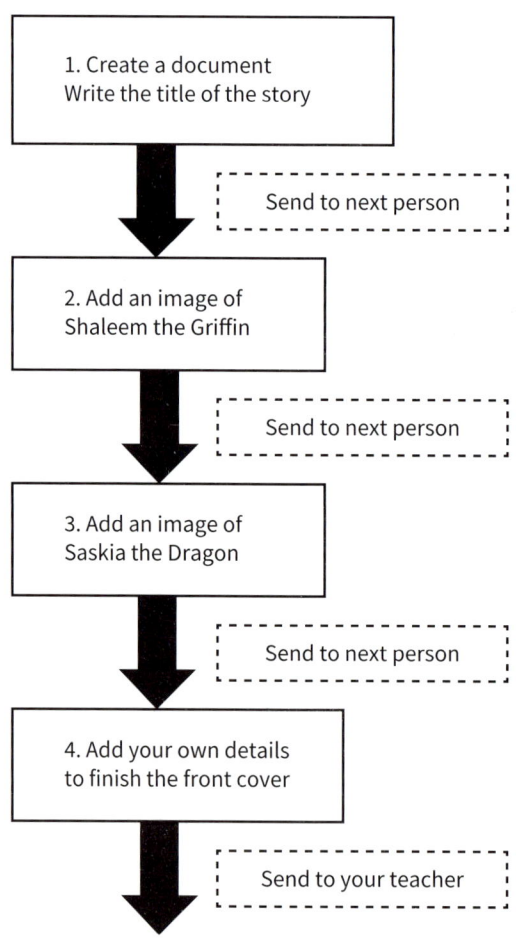

3 Exploring email

Reflection

1 Why is it important to read emails, and open attachments only from people you know?

2 Why is it helpful to keep your emails organised by using folders?

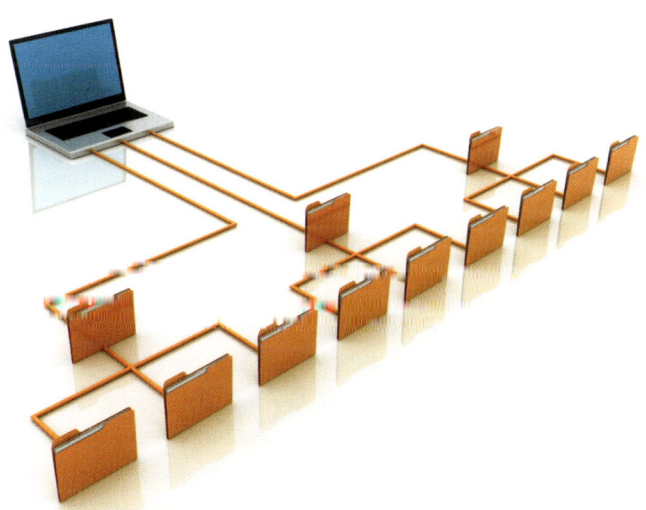

Exploring multimedia 4

	In this module, you will learn how to:	Pass/Merit	Done?
1	Create a page of text, images and sounds which use correctly named and positioned buttons	P	
2	Use effective page design	P	
3	Organise presentation slides with suitable choices and links	P	
4	Create pages that offer the user different routes through the presentation	M	
5	Show how the presentation meets the needs of your audience.	M	

> **Key word**
>
> **Audio:** another name for sound.

> **Did you know?**
>
> The word 'multimedia' was added to most English dictionaries in the early 1960s. That seems like a long time ago for a modern concept!

In this module you are going to develop skills to help you work towards your final project, which will be to create an exciting multimedia presentation using Microsoft PowerPoint. You could also use Keynote in iWork or other software that allows you to carry out the tasks detailed.

You will learn how to add text, images, sound (**audio**) to your presentation to make it exciting for your intended audience. This involves learning how to place items on the pages to make your presentation interesting and stimulating.

You will also be adding buttons to your presentation to help your readers find their way through it. These buttons will be created using hyperlinks.

Being aware of who your presentation is intended for will help you choose suitable fonts, colours and images to make it appropriate for your audience.

You will also learn how to:

- create a testing table to test your presentation.

4 Exploring multimedia

Before you start

You should:

- have word-processing skills that allow you to type text onto a page
- know how to use Microsoft PowerPoint
- know how to choose and change text and font styles, colours and images for different audiences
- know how to insert an image into a document and change its size.

Introduction

Multimedia is an exciting way to present information. It can come in many different forms and might include a mixture of text, graphics, sounds, images, animations and videos. It is the mixing together of these elements that makes a presentation 'multimedia'.

The use of multimedia on webpages and in presentations has changed the way people take in information. The addition of buttons and links means that readers can find their way through presentations in a way that suits them. This makes learning more effective and more interesting and can make creating a presentation a lot of fun!

The software that you will use to create your multimedia presentation is Microsoft PowerPoint. This is a specially designed presentation software that easily allows you to create presentation slides and add lots of exciting multimedia elements to them.

Multimedia needs to be used in the right way to make sure that it works well. You will learn some guidelines about adding multimedia to documents and how to make sure it looks formal.

WATCH OUT!

You must make sure that you get an owner's permission to use any text, images or sound in your presentation, that you have not created yourself. You could be accused of **plagiarism** if you don't.

Key words

Multimedia: a combination of text, graphics, sound, images and video to present information.

Plagiarism: using someone else's work but pretending it is your own.

Key word

Storyboard: a plan that you can create for your presentation.

Skill 1

Storyboarding a design

A **storyboard** is a very useful design tool that allows you to create a plan for your presentation. It is important to plan any presentation that you create, to make it look formal.

A storyboard is a pictorial representation of how your presentation will look. It allows you to plan the text, layout, formatting and multimedia that you will include in your presentation.

A storyboard is made up of several squares, with notes underneath each square.

The squares contain placeholders (boxes) that are labelled with the content that will appear on the slide, showing where it will appear.

The notes contain information about all the formatting and multimedia that will be included on the slide, for example any fonts and colours that are used and any animations, along with their timings (how long they last).

Activity 1.1

Open the document 'Storyboard_Template.docx' that your teacher will give you. This is a template that you can use to create a storyboard for a presentation.

You could use a computer to add the plan and the notes for each slide.

You could also print out the template and draw it by hand. Ask your teacher which of these you should do.

4 Exploring multimedia

Create a storyboard for a simple presentation about your favourite animal or maybe a pet that you have. Draw boxes to show where the text and images will be placed on each slide. Add notes to each slide to say what fonts will be used, what colours will be used, what animations will be used (along with their timings) and if any sound will be added to the slide.

Activity 1.2
Swap your storyboard with a partner and ask them to look carefully at your plan.

Ask them on a scale of 1 to 5 (5 being very confident) how confident they feel about creating your presentation from the plan that you have given them.

If they say 5, ask them to say what you have included in your plan that makes them feel confident. If they say 1, 2, 3 or 4, ask them what information is missing from your plan that would make them feel more confident about creating your presentation.

> **Tip**
> A storyboard should have enough detail so that if you gave it to another person, they could create the presentation in the way you wanted.

Skill 2

Choosing the layout and adding text to a slide

In Microsoft PowerPoint, each page in a presentation is called a slide. You need to learn how to add text to a slide but before that, you need to choose a slide layout.

To choose a slide layout, click on the **Home** tab and click on the **Layout** button.

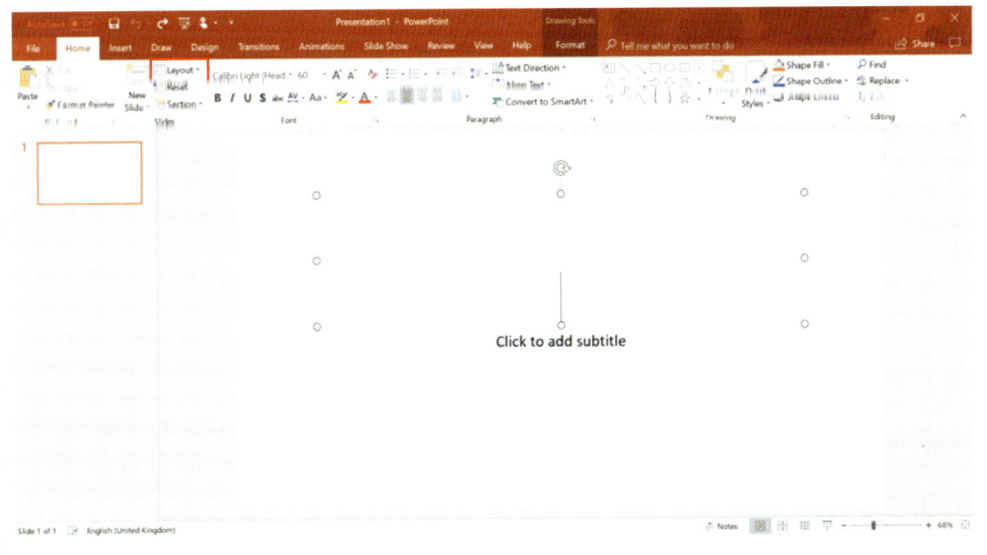

You will see a menu of different layouts to choose from. The two most commonly used layouts are 'Title and Content' and 'Two Content'.

For an introduction slide to your presentation you may choose to use the layout 'Title Slide'.

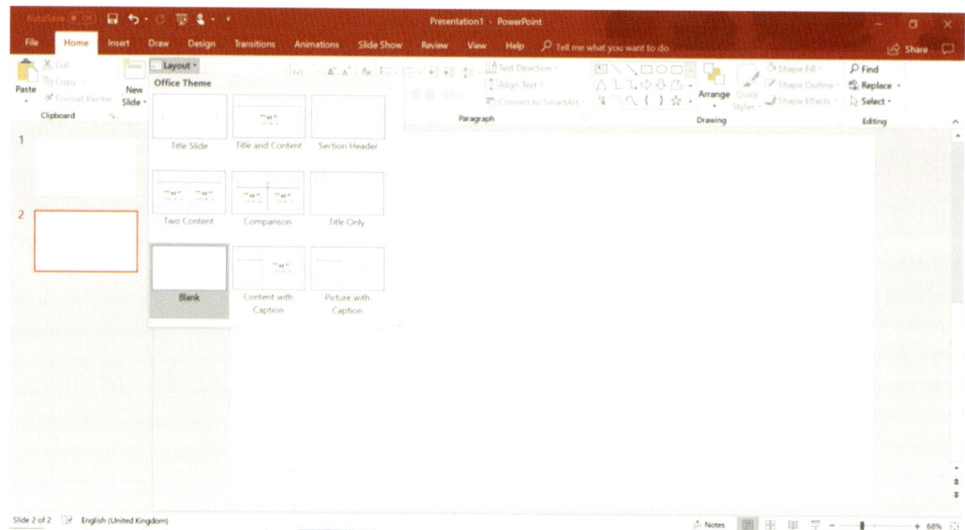

Tip

If you decide that you want to change the layout you chose, you can do this using the **Layout** button. You can do this at any time.

When you have chosen the layout that you want to use, you can click in any box on the slide and start typing to add text.

You can add a new slide to the presentation in two ways:

- Click the button that says **New Slide**. The new slide will have the same layout as the previous one.
- Click the little arrow on the **New Slide** button. This allows you to pick what layout you want for this slide.

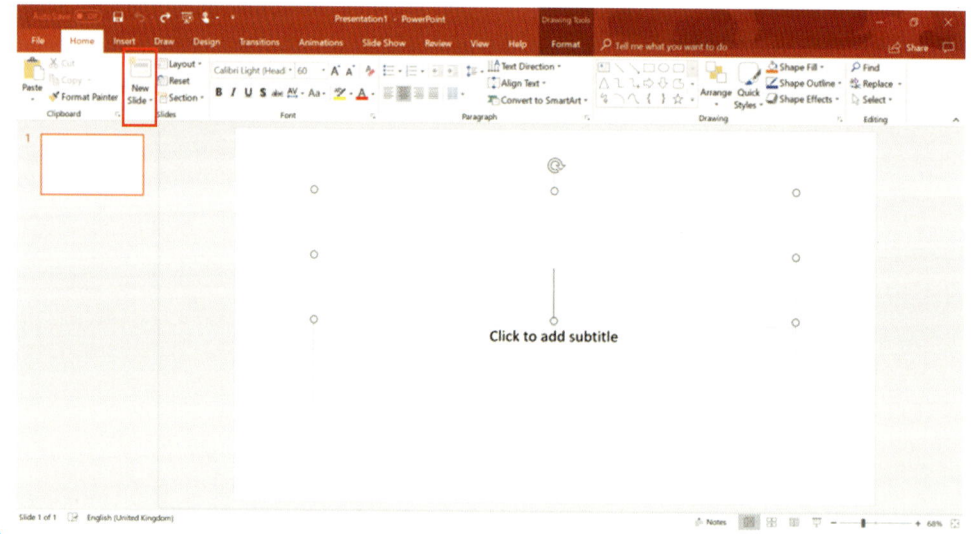

4 Exploring multimedia

Activity 2.1
Open a new presentation. Choose the slide layout 'Title Slide'.

Add a title of 'All about me' in the title box.

Add your name in the subtitle box.

Activity 2.2
Add a new slide to the presentation.

Choose the layout 'Title and Content'.

Add a title of 'My favourite things'.

Type a list of five of your favourite things into the main box.

Activity 2.3
Add a new slide to the presentation.

Choose the layout 'Two Content'.

Add a title of 'Things we eat'.

Type a list of fruit into the left main box.

Type a list of vegetables into the right main box.

Skill 3

Adding images

You need to be able to add and resize images to fit your presentation.

You can do this by opening a new presentation and selecting a layout.

To add an image you need to click on the **Insert** tab and click on the **Pictures** button.

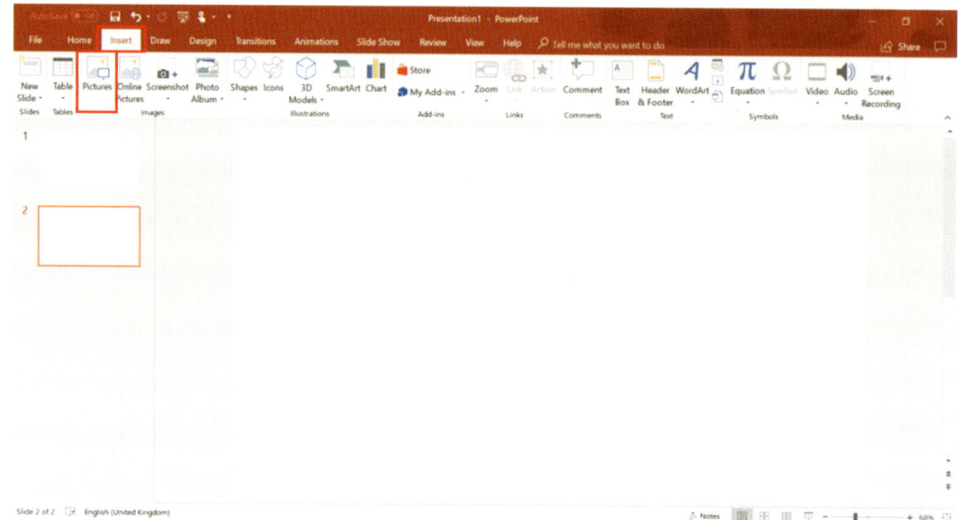

Find the picture that you want to add and click 'Insert'. You will now see the picture in your presentation.

To resize an image that you have added, click on the image and you will see a box appear around it.

By moving your cursor to a corner of the image you will see a double-headed arrow appear.

By clicking and holding the left mouse button, you can move your cursor towards the image to make it smaller, and away from the image to make it bigger.

If you need to move the picture around the slide, click on the picture and a box will appear round it.

Click and hold the cursor inside the picture and you will see a four-headed arrow appear.

You can now drag the picture to the place that you want it.

WATCH OUT!

When you are resizing an image, if you use the side of the image rather than the corner, you will make the image distorted.

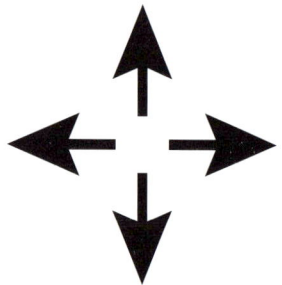

4 Exploring multimedia

> **Activity 3.1**
>
> Open the presentation 'Adding_images.pptx' that your teacher will give you.
>
> Add the image 'Robin' to the right main box on the second slide in the presentation.
>
> **Resize** the image so it fits.

> **Key word**
>
> **Resize:** when you change the size of an image.

Skill 4

Adding sound

When you add sound to your presentation, the software will add a sound icon and it will also add buttons to control the sound.

You can add sound easily by placing the cursor where you want the sound icon and buttons to appear.

When you click on the **Insert** tab and then the **Audio** button, you will see a menu that has two options:

- Audio on my PC
- Record audio…

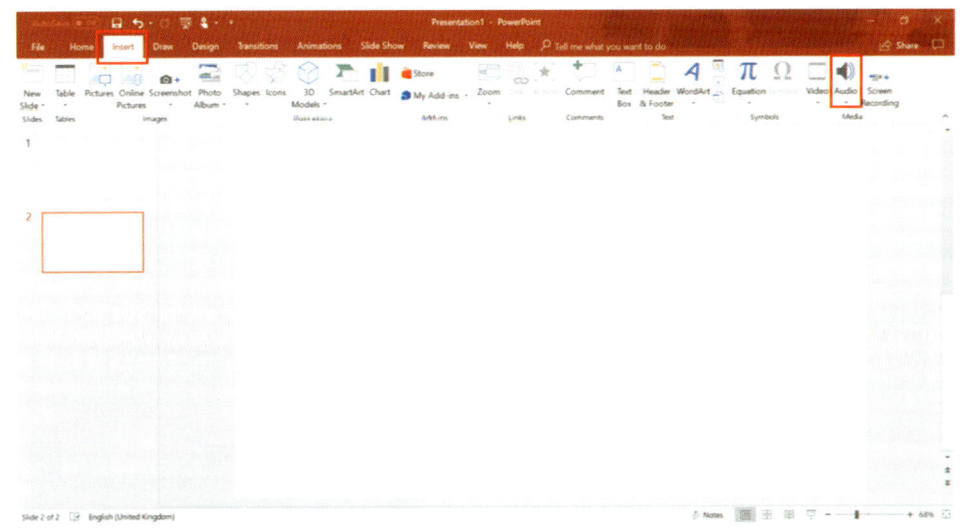

You can then click on the 'Audio on my PC' option.

You can click on 'Insert' once you have found the sound file that you want to add. You will see a sound icon appear.

If you move your cursor over the sound icon, you will see a 'Play' button appear.

You can click this button to play the sound.

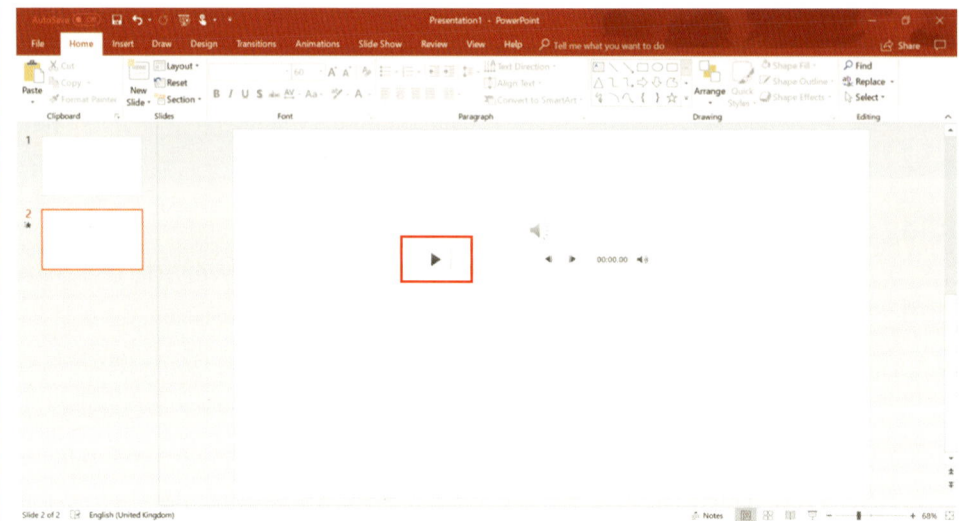

Activity 4.1

Open the presentation 'Adding_sound.pptx' that your teacher will give you.

Add the sound file 'Introduction' that your teacher will give you above the title 'Birds' on the title slide.

Skill 5

Creating a good design

The most important thing to remember when creating a presentation is the audience. You need to make sure that the presentation is clear and easy to read. You also need to make sure that the content of your presentation is suitable for the audience.

4 Exploring multimedia

Creating a presentation can be lots of fun. Adding lots of multimedia elements can be exciting, but if too many are added this can create confusion for the audience.

One thing to be careful about when creating a presentation is putting too much content on a slide. This could be too much text, using too many different colours, adding too many images or choosing too many different font styles. You should choose all these things carefully, making sure that they are suitable for the audience and purpose of the presentation.

There are guidelines that you can follow to make sure that you have a good design for your presentation. These are:

- **Do not have too many words on a slide**. Up to about 40 is a good number. Any more than this and the slide can become very messy and difficult to read.
- **Only use two different font styles.** You could use one font for the title and one font for the main text. If you use more than two different font styles, this can start to make it look messy too.
- **Do not use too many different colours.** You should try and pick a colour theme of three to four colours. If you use more than four, it can become too colourful, which can be distracting. You want the audience to be looking at the content and not all the different colours.
- **Use a simple background colour** that will not make it difficult to read the text.
- **Do not add too many images to a slide.** A good guideline is to have no more than two larger images or three smaller ones.
- **Make sure that images are not distorted.** Resize them correctly.
- **Do not add too many multimedia elements to a slide.** If a slide has text, images, video, sound and animations, this can be too much information at once for the audience to take in. You should think about adding a maximum of three multimedia elements per slide, for example text, an image and sound.
- **Make sure that all your slides have the same theme (fonts and colours)**. This will make your presentation look more formal and consistent.

Activity 5.1

Open the presentation 'Improve_me.pptx' that your teacher will give you. Discuss with a partner what the design issues are with the presentation. Make a list of these to show your teacher.

Use the guidelines given to improve the presentation and give it a better design.

You can change the design of the background of a slide by using the **Design** tab. See if you can work out how you do this.

Activity 5.2

Explain to a partner the changes that you have made to the presentation to improve it. In your explanation, tell your partner who the audience is for your improved presentation and how the changes that you have made are suitable for that audience.

> **Key words**
>
> **Navigation:** when you move to different slides in a document.
>
> **Linear:** when slides are linked in order, one after the other.
>
> **Non-linear:** when slides are not linked in order.

Skill 6

Adding linear navigation

You can make the **navigation** of your presentation **linear** or **non-linear**.

A linear presentation has buttons that will only allow you to move to the next slide, or the previous slide.

You can add this kind of navigation to each slide in your presentation using 'Action' buttons.

To find the 'Action' buttons, click on the **Insert** tab and then click on the **Shapes** button.

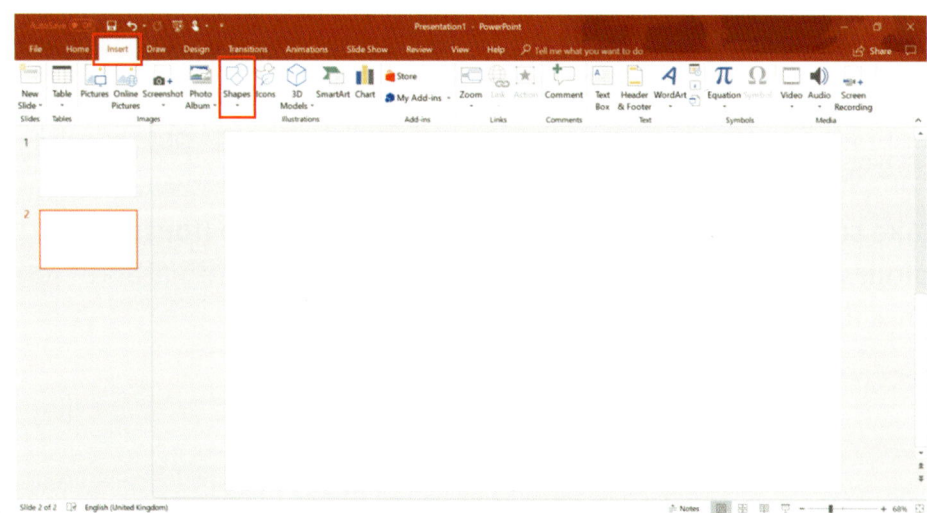

> **Tip**
>
> There is also a 'Home' button that takes you back to the first slide in the presentation.

4 Exploring multimedia

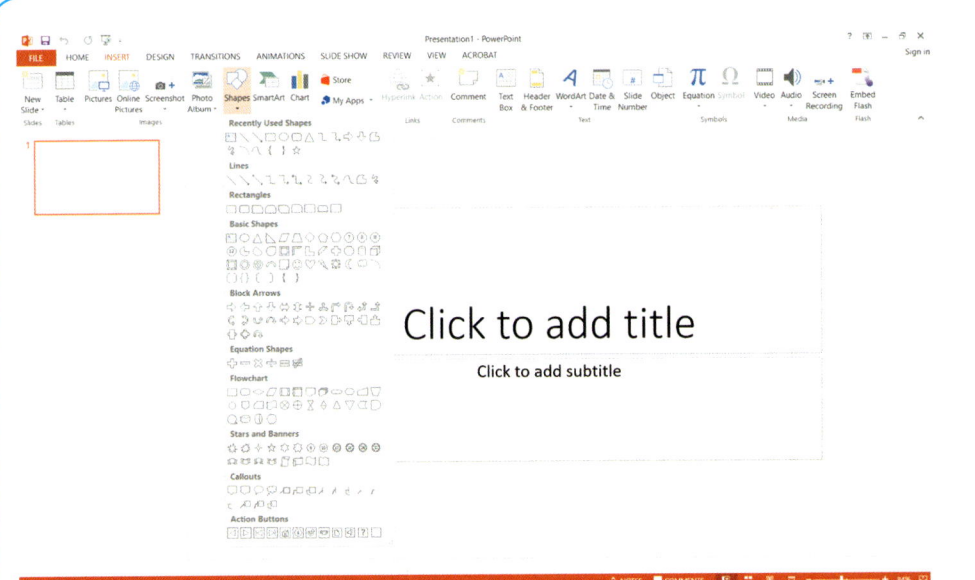

If you scroll to the bottom of the menu, you will see the 'Action' buttons.

	The 'Back' or 'Previous' button	This will let you go back to the previous slide
	The 'Forward' or 'Next' button	This will let you go forward to the next slide
	The 'Home' button	This will let you go back to the first slide

Action buttons are normally placed in the bottom right or bottom left corner of a slide. The buttons that are created use hyperlinks.

To add a button to go back a slide:

1 Click on the **Insert** tab and then the **Shapes** button.
2 Scroll to the bottom of the menu and click the ◁ button.
3 Move your cursor to the bottom left corner of the slide.
4 Click and hold the left mouse button and drag the mouse to draw a square shape for the button.

A menu will appear when you have drawn the button.

The button should automatically be set to 'Hyperlink to: Previous slide'. When it is, click 'OK'.

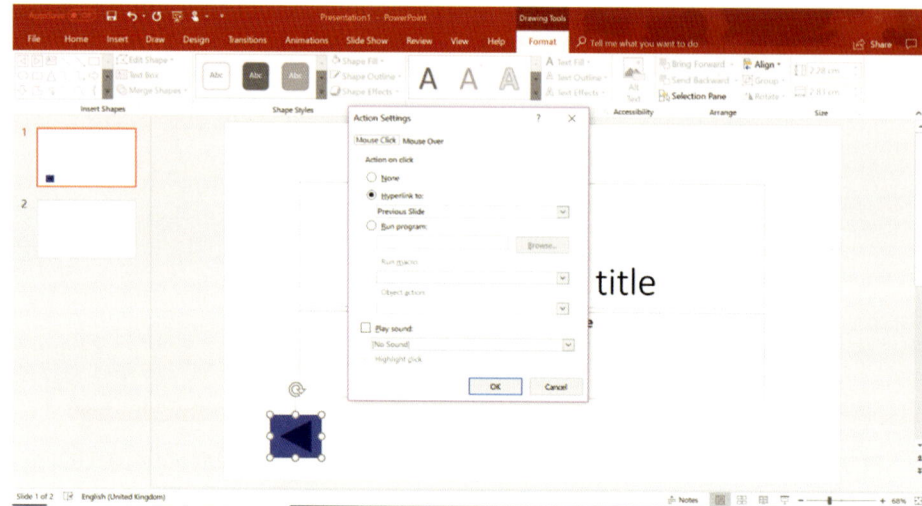

This will now set the button to move back a slide when it is clicked.

To add a button for the next slide or the Home button, choose the correct button and make sure that 'Hyperlink to:' is set to 'next slide' or 'first slide'.

Activity 6.1

Open the presentation 'Birds.pptx' that your teacher will give you.

On the title slide add a button to go forward a slide. Why does it not need any other buttons?

On the second slide, add a 'Home' button to go back to the title page and a button to go forward.

On all the other slides add a button to go forward, a button to go back and a 'Home' button.

Why is a 'next slide' button not needed on the last slide?

Save your presentation.

4 Exploring multimedia

Skill 7

Testing the Action buttons

To **test** if your buttons work you must be in 'Slide Show' mode.

To do this click on the **Slide Show** tab and select the **From Beginning** button.

Your presentation will go into Slide Show mode and your buttons should allow you to navigate your presentation.

You can move from 'Slide Show' mode to 'Edit' mode by pressing the 'Esc' key on your keyboard.

Activity 7.1

Open the 'Birds.pptx' presentation again.

Click on the **Slide Show** tab and select the **From Beginning** button.

Check that your Action buttons work.

Remember you can move from 'Slide Show' mode to 'Edit' mode by pressing the 'Esc' key on your keyboard.

> **Key word**
>
> **Test:** when you click something to see if it does what it is meant to do.

> **Tip**
>
> If you click on the screen during a slideshow, it might take you to the next slide without you meaning to. To stop this happening, untick 'Advance Slide On Mouse Click' under the **Transition** tab.

Skill 8

Adding non-linear navigation

A non-linear presentation means that you have buttons on each slide to move to any other slide in the presentation, and not just forward, back or 'Home'.

You can use text or a shape to create a hyperlink that will take you to a different slide in the presentation.

Using text as a hyperlink

To use text as a hyperlink, highlight the text that you want to use.

You can do this by moving your cursor to the end of the word and clicking and holding the left mouse button. You can then drag the cursor to the start of the word and stop clicking the left mouse button.

The text should now be highlighted.

Click the **Insert** tab and click on the **Link** button.

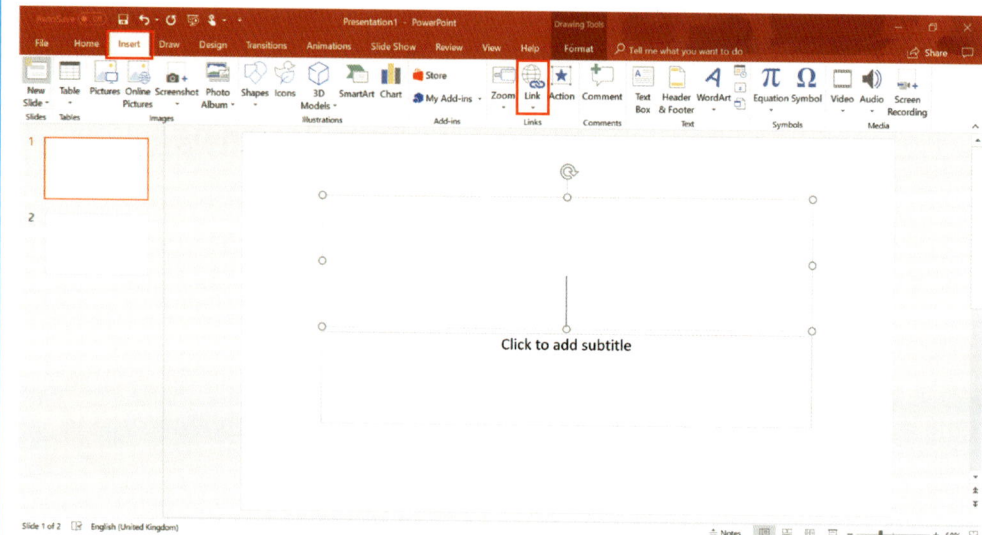

A menu will then appear.

Click the text on the left side of the menu that says, 'Place in this document'. Then choose the slide that you want the text to link to and click OK.

Using a shape as a hyperlink

You can use a shape as a link in the same way.

Click on the **Insert** tab and then the **Shapes** button. Select a shape and position it on the slide.

Click the shape so that it has a box around it to highlight it.

Then you can use the **Link** button to link the shape to another slide in the presentation.

4 Exploring multimedia

When you have added navigation to your presentation, you can check that it works as you wanted it to by playing the slide show. This will open your presentation into the full screen for you to look at and check. The button for this can be found on the **Slide Show** tab and it is the button that is labelled **From Beginning**.

Activity 8.1
Open the presentation 'Birds.pptx'.

On the second slide, highlight each text that is a bird and link it to the correct page.

Activity 8.2
On each slide that is about a bird, link the shapes at the bottom to the correct slides in the presentation.

Activity 8.3
Save the 'Birds.pptx' presentation. Click on the **Slide Show** tab and test out your links.

Activity 8.4
Write down who you think the audience is for this presentation. List at least two elements of the presentation (content, language, layout, colour or style) that you think are appropriate for the audience.

_____

_____

_____

> **Tip**
> Make sure you click on the shape itself to create the link and not the text within it.

Scenario

Out of this world!

Now that you have learnt the skills to create a presentation, you are going to create a multimedia presentation about space.

The audience will be children aged between 4 and 8 years old.

Your teacher will give you some text, images and sounds to use in the presentation. You will need to look at these and decide which are most suitable for your audience.

You will need to add navigation to your presentation.

Activity 1

Your teacher will give you a file called 'All_About_Space.docx'. Look at the text. Decide what text you think is suitable for your audience. You might want to change some of it to make it more suitable for the young audience.

Activity 2

Open a new presentation document and select design and style.

Add a title slide and give it the title 'Space'.

Add your name as a subtitle.

Copy the text that you have chosen into the presentation.

Make sure that you do not put too many words on each slide.

Give each slide a suitable title.

Choose a suitable font for the title and main text.

4 Exploring multimedia

Activity 3
Look at the images 'Space_1.jpg', 'Space_2.jpg', 'Space_3.jpg' and 'Space_4.jpg' provided.

Decide which two images are the most suitable for your audience that you want to include in your presentation.

Put the two images into suitable places in the presentation.

Remember to resize them appropriately.

Activity 4
Choose a suitable background for each slide in your presentation.

Activity 5
Add the sound file 'Countdown' to a suitable place in the presentation.

Activity 6
Add navigation to your presentation.

You could choose to add linear or non-linear navigation.

Activity 7
Save your presentation and check that the navigation works and that the sound file plays correctly.

Challenge

When you create a multimedia presentation, you should make sure that everything that you add is tested to make sure that it works properly. You can keep a record of this testing in a testing table.

Activity 1
Open the file 'Testing_Table.docx' that your teacher will give you.

Look at the example test.

Discuss with a partner what you think goes in each box.

Activity 2
Add another test for a different navigation button.

Activity 3
Add a test for sound.

Activity 4
Add tests for all the other navigation buttons in your presentation.

Tip

You may want to test things such as all the navigation links, to see if each link is correct. You may also want to test if the sound plays properly.

Final project – All about bees

4 Exploring multimedia

You are now going to create a multimedia presentation about bees. Your audience will be young adults. Make sure you create a good impression by making your presentation look formal.

Use the file 'Bees.docx' to help you.

Activity 1
Use the text given to you by your teacher to create your presentation. You could also use the internet to research further information about bees that you might want to include.

Activity 2
Use the internet to select suitable images to include in your presentation.

Activity 3
Include sound in your presentation. You could record a 20-second introduction about bees to add to your presentation. If this is not possible, your teacher will provide you with a sound to include.

Activity 4
Include 'Action' buttons for linear navigation through your presentation.

Activity 5
Make sure that you think about the audience of young adults when you are creating the presentation. Make sure that you follow the guidelines about good design.

Activity 6
At the end of your presentation, include a slide that is a list of the all websites that you used for any images and text in your presentation.

This is called referencing and it is what you should do for any text or images that you did not create yourself. This is to make sure that you are not plagiarising another person's work.

Activity 7
Ask a partner to test your presentation.

> **Stay safe!**
>
> When you are using the internet for research, make sure that you only use suitable websites that you can trust.

Reflection

1 Describe three ways that you have made your presentation about bees suitable for the audience of young adults.

   a _____

   _____

   b _____

   _____

   c _____

   _____

2 Describe how you would change your presentation to make it suitable for an audience of young children.

   _____
   _____
   _____
   _____
   _____
   _____

Acknowledgements

The authors and publishers acknowledge the following sources of copyright material and are grateful for the permissions granted. While every effort has been made, it has not always been possible to identify the sources of all the material used, or to trace all copyright holders. If any omissions are brought to our notice, we will be happy to include the appropriate acknowledgements on reprinting.

Thanks to the following for permission to reproduce images:

Cover image: *CSA Images/Getty Images*

RD Whitcher/GI; Scratch is developed by the Lifelong Kindergarten Group at the MIT Media Lab; Paul Seheult/GI; TimeStopper/GI; Jose Luis Pelaez/GI; Mekhamer Photography/GI; Kerstin Meyer/GI; Mario Tama/GI; Leonello Calvetti/GI; ANDRZEJ WOJCICKI/SCIENCE PHOTO LIBRARY/GI; Glow Images/GI; lvcandy/GI; PhotoHamster/GI; Bubaone/GI; Wulf Voss/GI; Sydney Bourne/GI; Alexsl/GI; YoungID/GI; Mysondanube/GI; Photographer is my life/GI; Adamkaz/GI; Jurgen Ziewe/GI; Photographer is my life/GI; Teunis Renes/GI; Flashpop/GI; Sciepro/GI; Kerstin Klaassen/GI; GlobalStock/GI; Mark L Stanley/GI.

Audio file: Larry Bryant/GI

Key: GI = Getty Images